Creating Your Dream Elementary Classroom from the Inside Out

What are the magic ingredients to a dream classroom and how can you create one for your own students? In this inspiring new book, Becky Hunt shows you how to transform the elementary school classroom into a special place where students are excited to learn. You'll gain practical strategies on key areas such as classroom environment, community, routines, procedures, expectations, lessons, and professionalism. You will discover how to:

- Design a classroom environment in which students feel safe, happy, and eager to learn;
- Arrange and facilitate regular class meetings so that students can express themselves freely, without judgement;
- Maintain professionalism in *and* out of the workplace;
- Set guidelines, rules, and expectations that students will understand and respect;
- Construct a targeted lesson plan with a clear beginning, middle, and end;
- Approach each day with a positive attitude by managing health and wellness;
- And much more!

Special features in each chapter include a "Tips from the Pros" section and "Reflect and Write" boxes to help you pause and apply the ideas as you go. There are also "Discussion Questions" and "Notes to Trainers and Mentors" so you can easily use the book for new teacher training, induction, book studies, and PLCs. With the practical tools and heartwarming examples in this book, you can have your own dream classroom starting today!

Becky Hunt is an educator, educational consultant, and children's author who has been the principal of both public and private schools. She specializes in teacher training and staff development, curriculum studies, international studies, balanced literacy, and leadership coaching and training. She is also author *of Global Concepts for Young People: Stories, Lessons, and Activities to Teach Children About Our World*. Visit her website at www.beckyhunt.net.

Also available from Eye On Education
(www.routledge.com/eyeoneducation)

Global Concepts for Young People: Stories, Lessons, and Activities to Teach Children About Our World
Becky Hunt

Your First Year: How to Survive and Thrive as a New Teacher
Todd Whitaker, Madeline Whitaker, and Katherine Whitaker

Passionate Learners, Second Edition: How to Engage and Empower Your Students
Pernille Ripp

The Passion-Driven Classroom, Second Edition: A Framework for Teaching and Learning
Amy Sandvold and Angela Maiers

Seven Simple Secrets, Second Edition: What the Best Teachers Know and DO
Annette Breaux and Todd Whitaker

Rigor Is Not a Four-Letter Word, Third Edition
Barbara R. Blackburn

What Great Teachers Do Differently, Second Edition: 17 Things That Matter Most
Todd Whitaker

The Genius Hour Guidebook: Fostering Passion, Wonder, and Inquiry in the Classroom
Denise Krebs and Gallit Zvi

Creating Your Dream Elementary Classroom from the Inside Out

A Practical Guide for Teachers

Becky Hunt

Routledge
Taylor & Francis Group
NEW YORK AND LONDON

First published 2019
by Routledge
52 Vanderbilt Avenue, New York, NY 10017

and by Routledge
2 Park Square, Milton Park, Abingdon, Oxon, OX14 4RN

Routledge is an imprint of the Taylor & Francis Group, an informa business

© 2019 Taylor & Francis

The right of Becky Hunt to be identified as author of this work has been asserted by her in accordance with sections 77 and 78 of the Copyright, Designs and Patents Act 1988.

All rights reserved. No part of this book may be reprinted or reproduced or utilised in any form or by any electronic, mechanical, or other means, now known or hereafter invented, including photocopying and recording, or in any information storage or retrieval system, without permission in writing from the publishers.

Trademark notice: Product or corporate names may be trademarks or registered trademarks, and are used only for identification and explanation without intent to infringe.

Library of Congress Cataloging-in-Publication Data
A catalog record for this title has been requested

ISBN: 978-1-138-58660-4 (hbk)
ISBN: 978-1-138-58661-1 (pbk)
ISBN: 978-0-429-50451-8 (ebk)

Typeset in Palatino and Myriad Pro
by Florence Production Ltd, Stoodleigh, Devon, UK

Contents

Meet the Author .... *vii*
Getting Started! .... *ix*

1 You Can Be a Dream Teacher 1

2 Design Your Dream Classroom Environment 13

3 Create Your Dream Classroom Community 39

4 Develop Your Dream Classroom Routines 55

5 Plan Your Dream Classroom Lessons 75

6 Keep Your Dream Classroom Alive 105

Thank-you Notes to Dream Teachers *123*
Acknowledgments *127*

Meet the Author

Becky Hunt is an educator, educational consultant, and children's author who has been the principal of both public and private schools.

Her most recent experience is as an advisor and trainer for government schools in both Abu Dhabi and Malaysia, expanding her international perspective in education. Presently, she is working as a trainer, advisor, and coach for schools in the area of literacy as an Education Support Specialist.

Becky has focused her career on helping schools to improve their strategies in teaching and creating nurturing environments where children come first. Her passion for helping teachers gain new strategies has helped to make a difference in the schools she has worked. Moreover, her global experience has broadened her insights by giving her exposure to great teachers in a variety of cultures enhancing the lives of the children they teach every day.

Her first children's book, *My Grandma's Crazy* (Ambassador International, 2014) is a tribute to today's grandmothers and a delight to both children and grandparents. Becky has visited many schools in the metro Atlanta area to share her book as a visiting author.

Areas of Specialization

- Teacher training and staff development
- Instruction and Leadership Coach-ICLE, a division of HMH
- Balanced Literacy Program
- International Studies
- Dual Language Bilingual program (English/Spanish)
- Educational Leadership—L-5 certification in Georgia

Becky is from Michigan and today lives in Atlanta, Georgia. Her daughter, Chelsea and her husband, Leslie, and her three grandsons, Mason, Carter, and Sebastian also live in Atlanta.

If you would like Becky to provide Global Concepts OR Creating Your Dream Classroom, training for your staff please contact her at, beckyhunt1@me.com.

Getting Started!

Hello! I am so happy that you have my book in your hands. You are ready to begin the journey to create your Dream Classroom. Like any journey, it is more fun when you take a trip with friends. Hopefully, you are using this book as a guide for professional development with other teachers and will be working with each other to provide support and share new ideas. However, if you picked up this book for yourself, go for it! I just encourage you to invite a teaching partner, your mentor, or coach, to provide support for you as you create your Dream Classroom, from the Inside Out!

As you read each chapter and work on the reflections and activities that are included, please take your time and don't rush. Rome wasn't built in a day, and neither is a Dream Classroom. This book is intended to be used as a handbook or a guide to support you throughout the process. Ideally, it is the start of the school year, and you will be able to begin the process before you ever meet your students. However, don't despair, if the school year has started and you weren't with this class on Day one. You will begin to create your Dream Classroom on the day you step inside your new classroom door!

I also want you to know that this is YOUR Dream Classroom, not mine! As an instructional coach, I will share with you my thoughts and ideas based on the experience and training I have gained over the years. My ideas will work, but I learn new ideas every day from teachers based on their own experience and personalities. At the end of each chapter, there will be a section called "Tips from the Pros." These tips will come from teachers, just like you, that have successfully developed their own Dream Classrooms. I encourage you to take my ideas, tips from the experts, and make them your own! Have fun with this book as you design and create your own Dream Classroom!

Becky Hunt

You Can Be a Dream Teacher

The teacher is the key to creating a Dream Classroom! The focus of this chapter is to help you to think back to the time in your school experience when you had a Dream Teacher. What made that teacher so special? Why did students love that teacher? What are the attributes of a Dream Teacher? Once you have identified the positive traits of your favorite teacher, you will begin to look at yourself and make a plan to become a Dream Teacher that makes connections with your students and makes learning for every student a dream come true!

Looking Back

Do you remember being a student in a Dream Classroom? It is very likely that your most vivid memory will be the Dream Teacher that created that classroom. Without a Dream Teacher, there will never be a Dream Classroom. It is the teacher who is the magic ingredient that makes a Dream Classroom come true.

My Dream Teacher was Mrs. Howard. I remember her voice as if she were speaking to me today. She was always so pleasant and calm. She smiled when she talked to us, and we loved her the first day we met. Mrs. Howard greeted us at the school doorway each morning and helped us to get our coats hung up and our lunch boxes stored before we went into the classroom.

Mrs. Howard began each day by reviewing the schedule and talking to us about the plans for our day. She encouraged and praised us on a daily basis.

She reminded us of her high expectations, but she never seemed to lecture or scold us. If we needed correcting it never took more than a raised eyebrow to get us back on track. Mrs. Howard taught us the basics, but she gave us plenty of time to read on our own and create unique projects. I remember designing our own kites and having a kite flying contest in March. In May, we made May baskets and hung them on the doorknob of friends and neighbors on our way home. We played softball in the spring. We prepared skits and songs for school programs that our parents enjoyed. And I remember listening to her read *The Long Winter*, by Laura Ingalls Wilder, on cold winter days after lunch. I loved school because I loved my teacher. I learned so much from Mrs. Howard, and I am thankful to her for modeling for me how a Dream Teacher creates a Dream Classroom. She showed us every day how much she cared for us, and she made learning meaningful and fun.

So now it's your turn. Who was your Dream Teacher? How did your Dream Teacher make you feel? What lessons did you learn? What made that teacher special? What attributes did your Dream Teacher have and what were the actions of your Dream Teacher that made him/her special? If you don't remember a specific teacher create your own idea of a Dream Teacher for the activity that follows.

Reflect and Write

Write your reflection and include details of your memories below.

My Dream Teacher . . .

Share your memories with your teacher partners. Together discuss the attributes of your favorite teachers and describe their specific actions. Based on your memories and reflections create a list of common attributes and actions of a Dream Teacher.

Attributes of a Dream Teacher	Actions of a Dream Teacher

Now it is time to think of yourself as a Dream Teacher. Which of these attributes and actions do you exhibit that makes you a Dream Teacher? Be generous to yourself and make a list of your best attributes and actions that you demonstrate in your classroom. Then list one or two that you want to develop!

My attributes	Attributes I want to develop

Now you have done some soul searching and have identified areas that you want to develop as you become a Dream Teacher. How will you make the changes needed? What potential roadblocks are there to implementing the changes?

Think this through and write an *"I Can"* statement to identify your goal. Determine an Action Step and write an *"I Will"* statement with steps to help you achieve your goal. Record your goals and action steps in the chart below.

Here is an example:

Goal:
I can greet my students and smile at them every morning when they come into the classroom.

Action Step:
I will have my lessons prepared so I can be at the door to greet them every day.

Goal 1	Action Step
I can . . .	I will . . .
Goal 2	**Action Step**
I can . . .	I will . . .

I recommend you start with two goals. Once you have mastered these, you can work on others if you choose. Creating good habits starts with consistency. There is no magic to being a Dream Teacher. Training, experience, and following your heart will help you to become the Dream Teacher you have always wanted to be.

Turn and Talk

Share your action plan together with a partner. How can you support each other?

Professionalism is an Important Key to Becoming a Dream Teacher!

Being a Dream Teacher is a full-time job. Once you have accepted the responsibility and stepped into the role of being a teacher, you will not only be a teacher at the school, but you will be a teacher at home and in the community. As teachers, we are role models and it is not just our students who are looking up to us. When you signed up to be a teacher you also signed up to be an inspiration to others, a guide, a beacon of hope to the world. You may be thinking, "Wow, that is asking a lot, I never thought of my role outside of school! When do I get a break?" Well here is the truth, and I am mentioning it because this is a lesson that I have learned over the course of a long career in Education. People do respect teachers. Most people would be the first to say they couldn't do our job! However, over the years views of teachers have changed, some say we have lost respect. But, there are some reasons for this, and some of us have not considered how our appearance, our attitude, and our communication skills have slowly chiseled away the respect people have for teachers.

Professional Dress

Dream Teachers come in all shapes and sizes. When I think back to the teachers I respected the most I realized they came in all shapes and sizes. I don't remember that they were fashion plates, but they all dressed professionally. It is essential to think about your appearance at school and present yourself as a professional. Your students, your colleagues, your administrators, and the parents are all watching and how you dress represents who you are and shows your professionalism.

When I first started teaching it was in the late 70s. I was a Flower Girl through and through. I had long hair and wore short skirts to school for my first teaching job. I was a 7th and 8th-grade reading teacher. One of my duties was to monitor inside a girls' bathroom between class periods. My first time on the job one of the girls pulled out a cigarette and asked me if I wanted one. I was shocked! "I am a teacher!" I said. The girls laughed and ran out. I realize now that I was only a few years older than those girls and I probably shopped at the same shops in the mall they frequented! After that day I started to work on a new wardrobe, and I even got a stylish haircut. I wanted to be recognized and respected as a teacher, so I had to make some adjustments to my style.

Your Life on the Web

Of course, it is not just your style that people will judge you by, it is your lifestyle as well. Social media has shown a wild and crazy side of society, please don't let your wild and crazy side show! Have you reviewed your Facebook page? How about your Twitter account? Everything that goes on Facebook reflects who you are, and how you live your life. Just be careful and sensitive to what you say and the photos you post on your Facebook page. We know some teachers have lost their positions because of words and photographs posted on their Facebook accounts, so don't let that be you. Be yourself and represent yourself honestly, but consider the messages you are sending out to the world!

Put in the Time

The first-year teacher has a big job to do, and it will take more than the hours of your contract to make your first year successful. The hours you spend before and after school organizing your classroom, preparing schedules, planning lessons, setting up your grade book, evaluating assessments, communicating with parents, and MEETINGS will consume your life. Any new job will take time to adjust to, but if you are a teacher in a new classroom and a new school, you have your work cut out for you. But here's the thing, it will make *your* life easier if you put in the extra time. The other thing I want you to know is, it will get better! I still remember the confidence and ease I felt during my second year of teaching. What a difference one year makes! So hang in there, you are striving to become a Dream Teacher, so you will feel pride when you look back at all you have done and the successes you have achieved!

Be a Team Player

Teachers are lucky because we have an opportunity to work together with our peers and colleagues every day. We all want to be on a great team, and it starts with being a great team member. Collaborating on lessons, projects, special duties, and just having fun together provides a web of support for everyone on the team. Just like you are getting to know your students, take time to get to know your team. Being part of a fun and hard-working, grade level team is worth its price in gold. Find ways to support your team and build a relationship with each one of them. I promise you that the payoff of being part of a great team is priceless.

Do the Right Thing

You have a teaching contract and a handbook to help guide you as a teacher. I recommend you read the handbook and become familiar with the routines and procedures for your school. A Dream Teacher comes to work on time, fulfills all of their professional duties, and supports the mission of the school and of the district. Your principal and leadership team depend on their teachers to do their job and always do what is best for students. Your reputation as a professional is determined by how you conduct yourself in your classroom, in the office, at meetings, and during professional development. Your professionalism will make you a valuable member of the school team.

Stay Positive and Focused

Finally, every school has teachers who have become negative, and sometimes they can be found in the teacher's workroom. When you hear negative talk about the school, the community, and even worse, the students, this should be your signal to leave. If you are in a school that has issues negative talk is not going to be the solution. I have worked in schools where I stayed in my classroom as much as possible to avoid being with the "Negative Nellies"! No school is perfect. Try to be part of the solution, not part of the problem. Real concerns and questions need to be addressed privately with school leaders.

Reflect and Write

Write a reflection about your role as a professional in your school!

Tips from the Pros!

At the end of every chapter, you will find a section called **Tips from the Pros**. The Pros are one of the finest groups of Dream Teachers, you will ever meet. The credentials of the educators in this group are incredible, but the advice they will share from their experience is worth its weight in gold. Each teacher generously participated in a Facebook Group I formed called Dream Teachers. As I wrote this book, I posed questions to the group, and they responded and dialogued with each other. I hope that you learn as much as I did as they shared their experiences, insights, and wisdom. Listen to what they are saying and strive to apply what you learn from each one of them as you are on your journey to becoming a Dream Teacher, like each one of them!

Tips from the Pros!

Question #1: How do you show your students that you care for them every day?

Anne-Marie I am always telling my students how much I believe in them and how capable they are!

Carole It starts at the door of your classroom, greeting every student with a smile and a "Good Morning!"

Claudia I tell them, or show them in different ways. Sometimes reading books and sharing your emotions with them. I was never ashamed to cry as a response to reading, *Love you Forever*, *The BFG*, etc. Showing them your love is the best way.

Vickie Knowing your students is key, their likes and dislikes. Meeting them where they are and always be the encourager. Celebrate successes and help them to work through their frustrations. Showing up at sporting events and recitals is icing on the cake!

Marcy I treat them as people first, students second!

Marion Know what students are interested in. Ask them about their families and their lives, even if you do need to write it down to remind yourself!

Bola My students used to always get a greeting at the classroom door with a smile!

Panzee Be consistent, fair, and prepared so each child can achieve success!

Erin I get down to their level and make them feel as important as they are!

Lynne Display student work and change displays frequently and be sure to include all students. Praise their individual efforts and results. Invite a peer to praise their work when students are in the room!

Question #2: What advice do you have for new teachers related to professionalism?

Lynne Read the Code of Conduct for teachers in your system. Ask questions to clarify your understanding. Act with honesty and integrity at all times.

Sharon With so much social media today remember your personal life needs to reflect professionalism.

Karen Be the teacher who shares resources, ideas, compliments, and encouragement. When other professionals in your building see your openness it can't help but come back to you ten-fold! Teacher collaboration opens doors for students. Let it begin with you!

Krista Never let your talent take you where your integrity can't keep you. Do the right thing when no one else is looking. Your students, their parents, and fellow teachers will admire you for telling the truth, admitting when you've made an error and acting in their best interest all the time!

Chelsea Ask yourself, will this help my students? If the answer is no stay out of it!

Katie Be super observant. Watch who's doing it right, who you admire. Emulate them until you find how YOU do it best!

Ann Marie Trust your instinct! Be humble and observant. Be a communicator. Don't stop learning. Be flexible and open to change and new ideas. Teach with your heart!

Dawn Marie Listen, listen, listen, stay clear of negative people.

Gail Watch, listen, and learn from students of all ages, teachers with years of experiences, and from families, too!

Marion Ask yourself if the people you are dealing with warm up or drain you of your positivity. Steer clear of the drains!

Claudia Professionalism starts from the top down. I had wonderful leaders in the early years who stressed being proactive, and gave us praise, even in the little successes! Teachers in turn do the same with their students. Earn respect and you will get respect. Continue to learn and try new methods. Sharing ideas with peers is always better than working alone! My favorite years were when our whole school worked and cared for each other as a family.

Isabel Find a mentor. Make a friend. I wouldn't have survived my first year in kindergarten without Cathy. She taught me so much about the things that really mattered and what I should focus on.

Katie Trust your instincts! Be humble and observant. Be a communicator. Don't stop learning. Be flexible and open to change and new ideas. Teach with your heart!

Marcy Here are a few:

- Prepare instead of repair, know your learners and plan ahead. Initially get to know each student on your own accord—not what another educator has determined, or what a learner's siblings or cousins did or did not do. Allow a new and organic relationship to form without the biases of others!

- Stay out of the lounge because it can be a toxic place in some buildings!

- Pay attention to the unwritten as well as the unwritten rules.

- Make decisions in the best interest of students and not what is easiest or the most efficient for you.

- Build relationships with colleagues

- Know when teaching is no longer for you.

- Take care of yourself.

- Know that the secretaries, maintenance crew, and cafeteria staff often know more about what is going on and the dynamics than the administrator! That being said—always defer to the administrator!

Discussion Questions

1. What is the most important message that you received from reading Chapter 1?
2. How do you want your students to remember you?
3. Why do students need to know that their teacher cares for them?
4. What are some barriers that you might face that could prevent you from connecting with your students? How can you remove them?
5. Why is professionalism so valuable to teachers and the teaching profession, especially in today's world?
6. Which quote from the pros really speaks to you? Why?

Notes to Trainers and Mentors

If you are leading a Dream Teacher group, provide a schedule and meeting time for the group members to follow.

Go through the Code of Conduct and School Handbook with teachers. Highlight areas of most importance with the group and explain as needed.

Discuss professionalism and expectations in the context of your school's culture. Expectations vary from different parts of the world, and even in different parts of a city. Religious observations, cultural differences, and community norms must be understood by teachers and staff to be successful.

If your school has a mentor program create a schedule for teachers to meet and define expectations for both the mentor and the mentee. If you don't have a formal mentor program, you may want to consider creating one.

Self Assessment

At the end of each chapter there will be a self assessment for you to check your progress and plan next steps!

Check the boxes that match you!

I am learning about my students and discovering more about them every day.	
I show an interest in what my students are excited about.	
I look for ways to connect with all of my students.	
I am a team player and growing professionally.	
I show my students that I care about them.	
I greet my students every day and show them that I am excited to have them in my class.	
I listen to my students and work together with them to solve problems.	

My Next Steps

Design Your Dream Classroom Environment

A Dream Classroom environment is essential to creating a classroom where children feel safe, loved, and excited to learn. How teachers use space tells a lot about how a they will approach teaching and learning. When desks are grouped in pods, students will be encouraged to work as a team and support each other. Cozy reading corners, nooks and centers indicate that students have freedom to move about the room and are encouraged to work independently. A carpeted area for students to gather as a whole group near the teacher creates a gathering place where the teacher can get up close and personal with students to teach special lessons, conduct shared reading lessons, and have class meetings. This chapter will describe the components of the physical space of a Dream Classroom and give you the opportunity to design the space in your own Dream Classroom.

Your Classroom is Your Home Away from Home!

Think about it. You and your students spend more time during the day in the classroom than at home. Your classroom is your home away from home. It is also home for your students. Just like your home, your classroom should feel warm and inviting. It should also make students feel comfortable and safe. The furnishing and decorations reflect who you are and show what you value. Your home is comfortable and nicely organized. Your classroom should be, too.

Our students come from a variety of circumstances, homes, and families. All children want to come to school and feel safe and happy in their classrooms. Unfortunately, for some students, this may be the only place they feel safe and happy. The time we spend creating a warm and inviting classroom environment is well spent. It is the first step to designing your Dream Classroom. It begins with designing the Space.

The Empty Classroom

You may have inherited a classroom from someone else or you are in the same classroom you had before. The first step is to really look at the space that you have. In the past, I have been assigned classrooms in old buildings and new buildings, large and small, and each have their advantages and disadvantages. No matter what size or shape your classroom is now, you can use the space and your creativity to design your Dream Classroom!

Take a close look at the space you have. Do you have storage? Cupboards? Shelves? How many bulletin boards are there? What kind of furniture do you have? Later in this chapter you will actually draw the space out on paper to use as a blueprint as you designate areas of the classroom for teaching and learning. Be sure and take "Before" photos. You will enjoy looking back at those early photos to see the progress you have made!

Here is a "before and after" picture from a classroom in Malaysia. With limited resources, and a limited budget, the teacher transformed his classrooms into a warm and inviting learning environment. Wooden desks and areas of the cement floor were covered with matching contact paper.

Resources are placed in centers for students to access.

Across the school teachers created reading corners and math centers for students to access books, games, and a variety of activities to support learning. All of which were made or purchased with limited funds from the school and their own money. These classrooms illustrate that it doesn't take perfect space and lots of money to create a Dream Classroom. It takes a teacher that is creative and resourceful to get the job done!

A creative teacher in Malaysia used a Space Theme for her classroom!

Creating a Classroom to Promote Literacy and Learning!

It is important for every teacher to create a classroom that supports literacy and learning. Your classroom environment is one of your greatest teaching assistants! Young children love learning and it starts when they enter the classroom door. A great teacher knows the importance of using space and color to motivate students to get excited about learning. The components of a Balanced Literacy Program are key to every elementary classroom. Creating space for whole group, small group, and independent instruction is the first step.

Arranging Student Seating

You may have desks and chairs, tables, or sleek modular furniture in your classroom. Whatever you have you need to make it work for you and your students. Think about your students first. Where will they sit? Where will they keep their coats and backpacks? Where will they keep their books and supplies for easy access? Consider where students will sit to see the board or screen for whole group instruction and presentations. Arranging desks into pods encourage cooperative learning and group work. This arrangement reflects a "student-centered" classroom. Desks in rows facing the front reflect a more traditional, "teacher-centered," classroom. How you arrange your classroom has big impact on literacy and learning. Look at your classroom and start to imagine where your learning areas will be located. Arranging your desks for student seating is the first step. Once you have your whole group desk area configured it is time to create learning areas in the rest of the classroom.

Carpet Area for Whole Group Instruction

Read Aloud Stories and Shared Reading lessons are best shared on the carpet at every level of Elementary School. Even students in Grade Five enjoy sitting on the carpet with their friends for important reading and writing lessons, mini lessons focused on skills, and class meetings. Students are more relaxed and focused when they are on the carpet. Teachers can make connections with students when they are close to them during instruction. Carpet time promotes togetherness and it is the best time to have class discussions.

Design Your Dream Classroom Environment ◆ 17

Your whole group carpet area should be placed in an area close to your White Board and/or Smart Board for lessons and interactive charting. Early Years teachers will want their carpet near their calendar area for calendar Math and other daily routines to start their day. Think about what you will need during this important instructional time and create a space for your chair and baskets of resources within an arm's reach.

Here are some resources you may need!

1. Whiteboards and Whiteboard markers for students.
2. Chart Paper and Markers
3. Books and resources for lessons
4. Sight Words

Small Group Instruction

Guided Reading or Small Group Table

A Balanced Literacy Program's key component is Guided Reading. Students learn to read best in small groups that are led by the teacher. Guided Reading groups are small so the teacher needs a round table or a U shaped table to conduct groups. Leveled readers and lesson plans, along with games, activities, and resources should be close at hand and organized on a shelf close to the teacher. A timer and a bell, along with markers, and other resources needed for lessons should be on the table. A set of whiteboards and markers, sight words, ABC Cards, and any other resources needed for small group reading lessons should be well organized and located at the table so there will be no wasted time during the precious hour of Guided Reading instruction.

The time spent at the Guided Reading Table with students in small groups is where the magic of reading happens!

Reading Corner/Classroom Library

Your class library and reading corner is one of the most important spots for independent reading. Elementary classrooms need a cozy reading corner where students can access books easily and enjoy reading. Your reading corner can be filled to the brim with a variety of books for students to enjoy. Your classroom library should include a rich collection of both informational and fiction books. Books can be grouped by topic, level, and interest. Pillows and comfortable chairs will attract students to the reading corner and encourage them to sit and read independently.

Developing your reading corner will take time and I promise you it will grow from year to year as you collect books from garage sales as well as your own friends and family. I encourage you to start your own personal book drive and ask people to donate new and used books. If you do be sure to give them ideas for levels and topics to get the "just right" books for your students. And of course when you select books for your classroom library make sure they represent the diversity of your students.

A cozy reading corner and a bright display of books will encourage your students to enjoy reading!

Curl Up with a Good Book!

There are many creative options for comfortable seating that I have seen in classrooms I visit. Teachers use bouncy exercise balls for students to sit in at their desks when they are wiggly. I have also seen a variety of portable chairs with backs that students can move around the classroom to read and work together in groups. Portable seating doesn't have to be fancy or expensive to provide a fun spot to sit and read!

Rub a Dub Dub, You Can Read in the Tub!

I have two friends who had the most creative reading spots for their reading corners that I have ever heard of. Vickie taught 5th grade and she had a bathtub filled with pillows that students could climb in and read a book. It was a comfortable spot to curl up and read and kids loved it! Vickie's students are grown up now and have children of their own, but they still remember Mrs. Winfield's Reading Tub!

Reading Dingy

Claudia, another friend of mine, shared her story about the dingy in her reading corner. She filled that dingy with pillows and students could climb in and read their books, pretending they were floating out to sea! They even called it the "Reading Dingy." I can only imagine how much students loved coming to school to enjoy reading in their classroom's "Reading Dingy"!

I am sharing these experiences to motivate you to think out of the box and get creative with your imagination as you begin to imagine your own Dream Classroom. Time spent in the front end of planning and creating spaces for learning in your classroom will have big pay off throughout the school year! You may not want to bring in a bathtub, or a dingy, but you may have a novel idea that will spark your students to enjoy reading!

Create and Sketch

Imagine what your Classroom Library and Reading Corner will look like. Draw a sketch of your vision below and label the items you want to put in your corner to create a space where students will want to come read!

Learning Centers

In addition to your Classroom Library and Reading Corner you will need a variety of learning centers to promote literacy and provide authentic reading and writing activities for students to do during the Guided Reading Block. You may have a large classroom and you will be able to designate specific areas for centers, or you may have learning centers in tubs or baskets that will be moved to tables when it is center time. For reading you will need three to four centers. Learning centers should be fun and focused! Students will want to go to the centers because the activities in each center are interesting and fun. If you have a 60-minute block for reading you will only need three literacy centers for rotations. Most teachers have an independent Reading Center, a Writing Center, and a Word Center, that may focus on phonics and spelling, vocabulary, and sight word activities and games. In addition to reading centers you will also want a Math Center and Interest Centers for Social Studies and Science.

For learning centers to be successful you will want to put into place important procedures and routines to help Center Time run smoothly. It is important to model for students how to use each center. Please know that I don't recommend you start the school year with every station set up and ready to go! The Class Library and Reading Corner start first. Once you have introduced the routines and expectations for Independent Reading time and using the class library you will be ready to introduce the next station. As you are thinking about the learning centers you want to have in your classroom, start thinking about how you will manage them.

Creating your Print Rich Environment

The walls of your classroom will become the second teacher in your classroom if you think carefully about what you want the walls to reflect. When I walk into a classroom where the teacher is using the walls to help teach I automatically know what is being taught because I can "Read the Walls." What I look for are the daily schedule, calendars, word walls, anchor charts, and interactive charts that have been done together with students. I also see wall space designated for different subjects that showcase student work. What the students are learning is evident in what is posted on the walls. If a class is doing a Space Unit, Leaders of the Civil War, or Scientific Discoveries that changed the world it is no mystery, because the "Wall" says it all!

Students use the walls as a visual reminder of what is being taught. Important examples of new learning are posted to help students to process.

As the units develop, the walls grow with charts, student work, posters, and a variety of examples of the learning that is happening in the classroom. Make sure to keep wall charts, student work, and displays current. When a guest comes into your classroom they should be able to identify current learning, rather than see what was done a month or two ago! Reading the walls is a wonderful thing for students because the walls reflect the important learning that is happening in their classroom!

You may want to start the year with a "Welcome Board." This board will get students excited about the start of the school year and help to bring your class together as a team. Your welcome board can be inside or outside of your classroom. Brainstorm an idea for a Welcome Board in the space below that you might want to create to welcome your students!

My Welcome Board

In addition to your Welcome Board you may want to feature some of the following ideas in your classroom's print rich environment!

Daily Schedule and "I Can" Statements

When students come into the classroom they need to know what they will be doing in school that day. Posting and reviewing the daily schedule and "I Can" statements is a great way to start off the day.

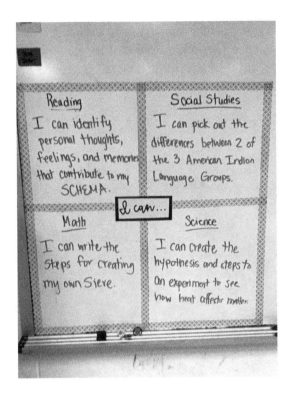

Once you have your schedule set it most likely will remain constant. The "I Can" statements will change once students have met that objective and the class moves to the next lesson. If you set the board up carefully on Monday it will most likely just need minor changes throughout the week. However, days where the schedule changes must be noted on the board and students need to be aware of those changes when you review the schedule in the morning. Students respond well to knowing what the schedule is and will remind you to follow it if you get off track!

Morning Calendar

In addition to the daily schedule and standards most teachers like teaching calendar routines to help children to learn important concepts in Math. Posting a calendar is a fun way to review the days of the week and the months of the year. Recording the number of cloudy, sunny, rainy, and snowy days shows students how to collect data and use that data to make charts and graphs. It is also important for students to know what day of the week it is and plan for events that are coming up in the future.

Keep in mind that your morning routines set the tone for the day and students feel secure when routines are in place. I love to see a teacher using the morning routines to set their class up for success! The 10–15 minutes used to prepare your class for the day is a great use of your instructional time!

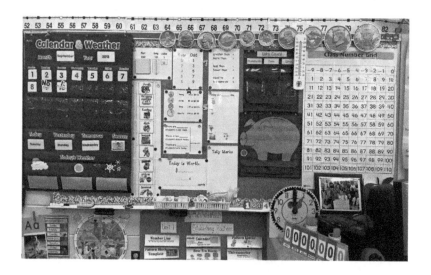

Word Walls

Word Walls can be one of the most valuable teaching tools in your classroom, however, they must be purposeful and consistently used to impact your student's vocabulary. There are many different kinds of word walls for you to consider. The most common Word Wall in grades K–2 are ones that build sight word vocabulary. As sight words are used they are placed on the Word Wall for students to refer to when they are writing and review and practice through a variety of games and activities. A Word Wall should be placed low enough for students to read and access. If wall space is an issue for you students can create their personal word walls in folders that they can use when they are writing. Word Walls can also be specific to content vocabulary that is being learned in Math, Social Studies, and Science. The most important thing to consider when you plan your word wall is how you will use it and where it will be displayed so that it is accessible to you and your students.

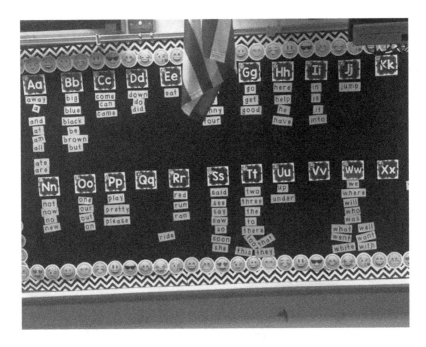

A Traditional Word Wall.

When students use the Word Wall is it a useful tool!

Charting

Charting is one of the most powerful instructional strategies you will ever implement in your classroom. Creating charts that are connected to important learning in the classroom will build your print rich environment and provide instructional clues to students as they apply their learning. Charting provides a significant path to gradual release as learning progresses from "I do" (the teacher). "We Do" (together with the teacher) and "I Do" (students work independently). Anchor Charts are done by the teacher to provide a visible clue and example for important strategies that are being taught and used in the classroom. Interactive charts are done together with students before, during, and after lessons. The important thing to keep in mind with charting is they are kept up in the classroom as a visual clue for students. They are a vivid reminder of what students are learning and they are useful to use as a reference during lessons and independent work. As students learn how to create charts with their teacher they will eventually be able to create charts on their own and in small groups to show their learning. The key to building your print rich environment is charting.

Anchor Charts—Charts created by teachers to use as an instructional tool and reminder of important learning strategies being taught and used in the classroom.

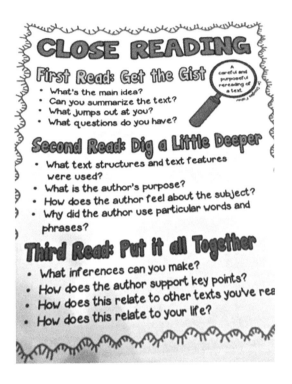

Interactive Charts—Charts done together with students to record learning before, during, and after a lesson.

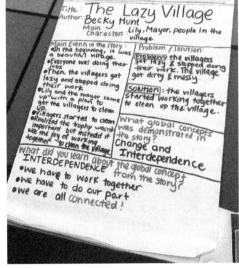

Create and Sketch—Design an Anchor Chart that you will want to use with your students starting the first day of school!

Creating the Mood

Students and teachers both do better when the classroom is cool, calm, and collected! Did you know that there are a few tricks that will help make that happen? Setting the atmosphere for learning is just as important as placing the furniture and organizing your classroom for learning. As you create your Dream Classroom, think about what cool colors you will use on the boards and the walls. Hues of blue, lavender, and a variety of pastel colors can be soothing and pleasant. Natural light is calming but even lamps can provide calm lighting in your classroom and will create a homey and cozy atmosphere. There are even light shades that can be hung on florescent lights to soften the strong glow that is on the ceilings of most classrooms. Adding some nice touches such as plants and pictures will make your classroom seem like home away from home. And nothing makes a classroom feel more relaxed than lovely soft music playing in the background during work time. Playing soft classical music is soothing to students.

Activity

Do a Google Search to get ideas for creating a calming classroom environment. Together with a partner look at the photos and read ideas from other teachers who have created a calm environment in their own classrooms. Jot your notes and favorite ideas below. Share your favorite ideas with your group!

Creating a Calm Classroom Environment!

Just say NO! to clutter!

We have all had a bad day or two when things got away from us and our house became a bit cluttered. But when this happens in a classroom it sets a very negative atmosphere for learning. Students cannot learn in chaos and clutter. Disorganization in the classroom leads to chaos!

When I was a student teacher I learned a very important lesson. My supervising teacher, Mrs. Jones, called me at home and asked me to come in early to class the next day. She said we had a "Project" to do. I was quite curious about what this "Project" might be.

When I went into the classroom the next day Mrs. Jones walked me around the classroom to show me where I had left my mark around the classroom. I had scattered a variety of books, papers, crayons, markers, and other various items I had used that day all around the classroom. I left items on shelves,

Don't let your classroom become cluttered!

book cases, cupboards, desks, and chairs all around the room. I was so embarrassed! Mrs. Jones had been to the store and she gave me four dish pans and my own shelf to organize my teaching supplies. She taught me an important lesson that day. She said, "If the teacher isn't organized, how can we expect our students to be organized?" She was so right and I took that lesson to heart. My classrooms and offices for many years after were well organized. I created a system that worked for me and my students so that my classroom ran like a well-oiled machine. Organization starts when you are creating your Dream Classroom. Think about where you will store your resources, teaching guides, books, art materials, paper, and everything else a teacher has to store in the classroom.

Don't let your classroom become cluttered!

Organization is Key!
This organized teacher has her Guided Reading supplies organized and located next to her Guided Reading Table. Everything she needs are in the drawers, including a drawer for each Guided Reading Group with their levelled readers, lesson plans and assessment records!

Find a place to store resources and materials. Take time at the end of each day with your students and by yourself to put everything back into place and prepare for the next day!

Classroom resources that are accessible and stored neatly get used with care and they are easy to return to the right spot!

Assignment—Design your Dream Classroom!

Now it is time to design your own Dream Classroom! Your head is spinning and you need to put your ideas on paper. I suggest you draw your classroom to scale to use as a guide to follow as you develop your classroom environment. If you already have your classroom you can draw in your windows, doors, cupboards, and shelves. If you don't have your classroom assignment design your Dream Classroom and let your imagination go wild! Here is an example.

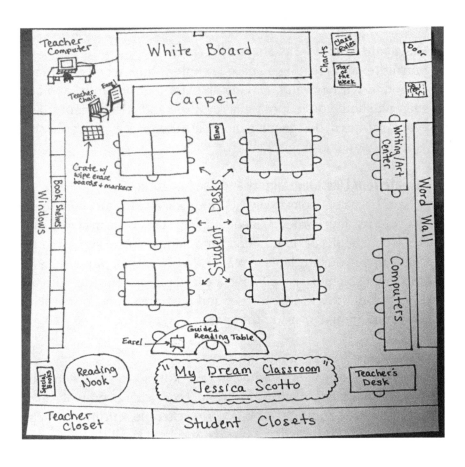

Creating Your Dream Classroom—Step by Step!

You have a beautiful design for your Dream Classroom. Now the hard work is ahead of you as you put those ideas on paper and turn it into a reality. Teachers spend many hours behind closed doors creating their classroom environment. This is important time spent because you are creating space for your students to learn.

Step 1—Get rid of the Junk!
The first step for me was usually to clean the room out of the junk I wasn't going to use. You may wonder why I say "junk." It is because I often inherited classrooms that were full of old textbooks, broken furniture, broken equipment, and boxes of outdated resources. If this happens to you I recommend that you ask a colleague or a friend to help you! It is also a good idea to be aware of what curriculum and materials you will need so you don't throw out important resources! It will feel good to "purge" the room. Remember, it's your Dream Classroom, and this is the first step to make it your own!

Step 2—Set up the furniture and arrange the space
Moving furniture and creating a space is another time when you may want to work together with a friend. Having an extra pair of hands, and an extra pair of eyes, will help you to locate the furniture and create beautiful spaces. Refer to your classroom design map and create the space where your students will be working and learning together.

Step 3—Create Your Classroom Library and Reading corner
You may have boxes of books to unpack, or just a few to start with! It doesn't matter, get your reading corner created. Organize the books in colorful baskets and bins. Display books of high interest and hang colorful signs and posters that will encourage your students to read. Add in a carpet, pillows, and chairs if you have them so children will have a cozy space to curl up with a book. Post a sign or label the Reading Corner and post directions for checking out books and expectations for using the space.

Step 4—Create your Print Environment
Think about your students and what you want them to see when they first enter their classroom. Begin with your front board where you will start every day with the daily routines. List your daily schedule, outline the space for the I-Can statements, and display your daily calendar routines.

The next area I would create is the Word Wall. Think carefully about its location and how you will use it. Most teachers want it placed at the front of the classroom to use as part of their routines. Wherever it is make sure it is accessible to students and easy to review with the whole class. The Word Wall will start with a few words and as they are introduced the Word Wall will grow.

Start the year out with your welcome board and also create a special board or area on the wall to display student work. You may also want to start with one or two anchor charts that are focused on important skills you will be introducing at the beginning of the school year. Keep in mind that the goal is to be strategic as you build your classroom environment. The last step is to create labels for each area of the classroom so students know what the spaces will be used. Finally, don't think you need to fill every space. Students will become overwhelmed in a classroom that is too busy and has too much print on the walls.

Starting the year with your print environment:

1. Daily Schedule/I-Can Statement/Calendar area
2. Word Wall
3. Welcome Board
4. Student Work Display Board
5. Anchor Chart
6. Classroom Labels

Acquiring Resources on a Shoe String Budget!

You may be a lucky teacher that works in a school that has lots of great resources for your classroom environment. We are happy for you if that is the case! However, most of us have had to be very resourceful to get what we need for our classrooms. And sometimes it isn't what we need we can't get, but what we really want that we don't have funds for. Where will the money come from for comfortable chairs, books, plants, lamps, bulletin board borders, chart paper, markers, and the list goes on! Most teachers spend out of their own pocket for what they need in their classroom, and I have seen this in every country I have worked! Teachers around the world spend from $100.00 to $1,000, and more, of their own money for resources. Yikes, that is a lot of money for a professional to spend, especially because educators are paid so little!

Here are some ideas for you to start a campaign to get the resources you need to create a fabulous classroom environment for your students!

1. Just Ask
   I have discovered that people are very generous when they are asked by someone they know and love for help! Reach out to your family, your friends, your church when you have needs. You will find all kinds of resources if you ask! Here are some examples of good "Asks" for people you know. *"Do you have any comfortable chairs, carpets, lamps, baskets, or bins or children's books that you could donate to my classroom? I am creating a Dream Classroom, environment that will encourage my students to read and learn."*
2. Garage Sales and Thrift Shops
   New teachers are always looking for books for their classroom library so don't be shy about asking for support. Scout around your neighborhood's garage sales and thrift shops. If you find items for your classroom library like books, bins, shelves, ask the owner of the sale if you could get them for free or a good discount for your classroom. Most people are wanting to get rid of stuff so this is a good place to start.
3. Book Drive
   I also recommend having a formal "Book Drive." Use Social Media to get the attention of people connected to the school to donate books to your classroom library. Give them ideas of what you are looking for so you get good quality books! Ask your school family, PTO and your own class to help you to build your class library! Children will feel good about bringing in books they are finished reading and add them to the class library! (Pictures books, chapter books, favorite authors, non-fiction topics, etc.)
4. Neighborhood Business Partners
   Hopefully your school has built a relationship with businesses in your community. If not, you can approach them yourself to ask for supplies, treats from the grocery store for class parties, Paint chip samples, carpet samples, and anything else you can think of that you could use in your classroom!
5. Grants
   In the United States there are several grant programs for teachers that are funded by a variety of sources, including local citizens and businesses. I good grant can get funded in a hurry if you show the need and how you will use the funds. One in particular that we love in the U.S. is "Donors Choose." This grant source is only for teachers! Do some research and find grants in your community and in the nation for you to apply.

6. Scrounge
   Every school I have ever worked in has a storage room filled of wonderful "stuff," that I would drag to my classroom and use. Books, old AV equipment, games, activities and even furniture are often chucked away in storage rooms and forgotten! Ask your principal for permission to check out the storage room for items you may need for your classroom. And watch those hallways for items your colleagues are finished using.
   Remember, "One teacher's junk, is another teacher's treasure!"

Use Your Magic to Create Your Dream Classroom!

You have designed your Dream Classroom environment and now you have a plan. The thought and work you have put into your classroom will have big pay off as you start the school year. There is magic in the work you will do to create a beautiful space for learning that not only will inspire your students to learn, but also reflect your personality and sense of fun! Unfortunately, there is no magic wand to wave to create your Dream Classroom environment. It will take many hours of hard work.

I suggest you talk with your principal and get into your classroom a few days before school starts. The professional development and staff meetings that you will be expected to go to will give you the direction that you need to start the school year. If you have your classroom ready you will be able to focus! Good luck to you as you create your Dream Classroom environment. And remember, it is a work in progress. Have fun and create your magic!

Tips from the Pros!

What advice do you have for teachers setting up their classrooms?

Vickie This place you create will be your home away from home for you and your students. Please make it feel like a place you will want to live and learn together!

Dawn Be sure that the movement patterns are good. You need to be able to get around to every student where they work. Placing the furniture is important. If you are a new teacher, you may want to group tables in pairs. Teaching students to work in pairs before working in larger groups is much easier before moving them into groups of four.

Chelsea Set up the furniture first. Do not start unpacking! Look at the room. Is it working? Is there a better place for something somewhere else?

Lynne Make signs and labels for areas and items that are in the room. Laminate labels so they can be reused and moved depending on the changing environment. Add images to signs and labels. Multi language labels may also be relevant in your classroom.

Isabel Check out your teammates' classrooms.

Gail Leave plenty of space for students to make it their own.

Ann Marie Be open to changing things once the students get there.

Eliza Stand on your knees in the middle of your classroom and make sure everything is on the children's eye level!

Tina I think it is still important to have a carpet area for class meetings, even in upper elementary classes.

Katie Put supplies such as crayons and pencils on shelves low enough so kids can get them without help from the teacher! Store supplies you don't want students to get into up high, out of reach!

Discussion Questions

1. What did you learn about classroom environments that was new for you?
2. Did you discover some changes you want to make in your classroom design that will make a big impact on students' learning?
3. What are some obstacles you think you may have to creating your Dream Classroom? How will you overcome those obstacles?
4. What are some "Tips from the Pros" that you're going to use?

Notes to Trainers and Mentors

Supporting teachers as they plan and develop their classroom environments is time well spent. Work together with teachers, or assign them a partner to provide them with another pair of hands to set up the classroom, create centers, bulletin boards, and cozy learning spaces. It is fun and exciting to set up a new classroom and often it takes two pairs of eyes and a partner to get a classroom ready to welcome an eager new group of students!

Self Assessment

Check the boxes that match you!

My classroom environment is warm and inviting.	
My classroom is a print rich environment.	
The books and resources in my classroom are accessible to students and well organized.	
My classroom has a cozy reading corner with a class library for independent reading.	
My classroom environment is a calm learning environment.	
My classroom has areas for whole group, small group and individual instruction.	
My classroom is organized and free of clutter.	

My Next Steps

Create Your Dream Classroom Community

Every child wants to belong. It is that simple, isn't it? Children learn best when they are part of a caring community at home and at school. While we can't control what happens at home, we sure can control what happens at school! What is your vision of your classroom community? Does the picture of a family come to mind? I am sure it does and that is definitely the direction we want to go with our classroom community. It all starts with you!

Creating your classroom community is one of the most important steps to creating your Dream Classroom. You have spent hours creating your Dream Classroom environment. It looks, beautiful. But esthetics is only part of a Dream Classroom. What does you Dream Classroom *feel* like? What does your Dream Classroom *sound* like? Close your eyes and imagine your dream classroom environment. What are the children doing? What are you doing? Is your classroom community kind to each other? How do children and the teachers speak to each other? Do children feel safe? Do they feel loved and cared for? Take time to imagine what your Dream classroom looks like, feels like, and sounds like.

Reflect and Write

Think about your idea of a Dream Classroom environment. Record your thoughts below. Share your ideas together with your partner.

My Dream Classroom *Looks* like . . .

My Dream Classroom *Feels* like . . .

My Dream Classroom *Sounds* like . . .

Now that you have a picture of what your Dream Classroom *looks* like, *feels* like, and *sounds* like, think of this as your goal. Every step that you take toward building your classroom community and making meaningful connections with students will help to make the picture you have created in your mind, a reality. As you read through this chapter and plan your Dream Classroom community keep your goal in mind!

Building your Classroom Community

You can take purposeful steps to create community for your classroom before school starts. Think about it, how will you greet students and make them feel welcomed the first time they visit? How will you make students feel like they are part of your team? What can you do to make each child and family feel like part of the community? Your classroom should feel like a family. Creating a family feeling in your classroom is the most important step you can take as you create your *Dream Classroom* Community.

My favorite way to start school was to create my own classroom name. My students were "Hunt's Heros." Outside of my classroom was a Welcome Board with our class name. At our first class meeting I introduced myself and led a discussion about what it means to be a Hero. We brainstormed and I charted the super powers of "Hunt's Heros." Of course they came up with all the right ideas! Hunt's Heros are "SMART, KIND, RESPONSIBLE, CARING, HARD WORKING, etc."

To complete the Welcome Board, we used paper cut outs as a model and each student created their own Hero! Students loved designing their Super Hero and I displayed th:em on the board outside of the classroom with their name. One year I even designed a t-shirt for students that I purchased with a mini grant. Students loved wearing their t-shirts and they were great for special events and field trips. My students loved being a Hero and they were proud to be together in our class. We were a little family, we cared about each other, we worked together, sometimes we had to work out our differences, but at the end of the day we were a team.

So think about it? What would be a good name for your classroom? How will that name bring students together and guide them as a team? Brainstorm some ideas for your classroom name below. Once you have your class name list some ideas of how you will use your class name to bring your class together as a team. What are some fun activities, games, boards, and ideas for you to use in your *Dream Classroom?* Use the space below to job down your ideas!

My Classroom Team Name	Lessons and Activities to Create your Classroom Team!

So now you have your Classroom Team Name and you are preparing for the first day of school. This is the most important day of the year. The appearance of your classroom, your welcome and greeting to each student and the activities of the first day set the tone for the year. Your approach to the first day is essential to creating your classroom community. The planning and preparation for this day will make the first day go smoothly and your students will be excited about their new classroom and their teacher! Give your students a positive first day and that day will set each student up for a great year!

Ideas to get started:

1. Call students or send them a post card to welcome them to your class before school starts.
2. Create a Welcome Board with your team name outside of your classroom.
3. Write a Welcome Letter for parents. Include a little bit about yourself, essential information about the classroom, homework process, contact information, and invite them to write you a letter about their child.
4. Put students' names on their desks or tables so they know where their space is when they come into the classroom.
5. Create a Community Meeting center in your classroom.
6. On the first day and every day greet students at the door! Shake their hand, introduce yourself, and welcome them to the class.
7. Start the first day with a class meeting to develop the class team.
8. Create the Team Characters for the Welcome Board.
9. Have fun with your class with team building activities.
10. Goal Setting—My hopes and dreams for this school year!

These are some ideas for you to try, and I am sure you have more great ideas. The important thing is for you to make sure that every student leaves your classroom and goes home with a positive feeling about the first day. You will definitely make parents happy if their children go home and report that they made friends and had a great first day. If they report that they like their teacher, you have hit a home run on the first day of school!

Supporting your Community with Class Meetings
Building community with your class starts on the first day and continues throughout the school year. Keeping your class motivated to work together and creating a positive family feeling will need nurturing throughout the school year. Students grow and change, new students are added to your class, and events can take place that will impact your class that can take away that feeling of community. The best way to keep the positive energy going all year long and teach important social skills is to have class meetings.

Greeting each student every day as they enter the classroom sets a positive tone for the day. Gathering in the community area is also a great way to start your day as you welcome students and review the morning calendar, the schedule and events for the day. Some mornings you may want to have class meeting to meet the social-emotional needs of your class.

Class meetings are a great way to start off the school year to focus on the changes that students are facing as they start a new grade. Making new friends, starting a new school and changing grades are challenges students face every year. Class meetings can help students to feel comfortable with these changes through a variety of activities to get to know each other. Playing games together, learning each other's names, singing songs, and listening to stories about starting school, making friends, and being kind to each other will help your students to become friends and work together. As your Dream Classroom community grows and changes throughout the year you will discover additional topics you want to explore with your students. Bullying, celebrating diversity, and emotions are some topics that you may want to address. Also, class meetings are a great time for students to voice their own concerns and you want to create an atmosphere of trust and non-judgment so students will feel comfortable sharing in an open discussion.

Together with the students create a list of norms or expectations for behavior during class meetings. Some ideas they will most likely come up with are, "Listen to each other, Don't interrupt, Respect each other's ideas, Encourage and support each other." Create an anchor chart with these norms listed and refer to them before you start your class meeting and throughout as needed. Class meeting time is a time for students to be able to express themselves and their feelings without judgment from others. These norms will continue throughout the school day with your students as you practice them throughout the school year.

How Often Should I Have Class Meetings?

Ideally you will meet with your class to start the day and go through the morning routines daily. At the start of the school year I would take time every day to build community through games, activities, and a Read Aloud story. A little bit a day will go a long way toward creating your Dream Classroom community. As the school year goes on you may want to designate certain days to focus on social-emotional needs of the students and the class. Also, as things come up in your classroom that become issues you may want to add an additional class meeting to discuss and problem solve during the school day.

Class Meetings are not Counseling Sessions

As a classroom teacher you are building community with students by teaching them important life-skills. Being kind, being a good listener, being a friend, working together as a team, are all common themes for class meetings. I do want to caution you not to allow the session to turn into personal drama and issues for individual students, or small groups of students. There may be times when you want to speak to students privately if they share issues of concern. I also recommend that you alert your school counselor and parents if something comes up that you are concerned about!

The most important reason to have class meetings is to make connections with your students. Making that personal connection with students through discussions and sharing during class meetings is the most important key to creating your Dream Classroom environment. *You* are the key to creating your Dream Classroom and class meetings will help you to make that happen!

Having Fun in Your Dream Classroom!

Here is a photo of me being Silly with kids as I share my book, *My Grandma's Crazy*.

Having fun with your class is the best way ever to relieve stress and make memories with your students! When your students see you as a fun teacher who can have fun and be silly with them they will love you forever. Here are a few "Silly" ideas that will make learning fun in your classroom!

Play Music

Your students will learn how to be a team and work together when they are having fun! In fact, your students will learn academics at a higher rate and with more understanding if they are enjoying their lessons. School should be fun and it is your job to make it fun! Nothing brings more joy into a classroom than music. Playing music when students are in the classroom can really set the mood and bring your classroom community together. Singing songs together is fun and students love to sing together! Games and activities are not only educational, but they create a positive experience for students as they learn to take turns and play fair.

Play Games

Students learn from playing board games together. I often had "Game Day" on Friday afternoon to celebrate a great week of learning with the class. I also had a puzzle table where students were free to go and work together to put together a puzzle. All of these activities provide an enjoyable experience and they will motivate your students to become a team as they work and play together. Developing you Dream Community has so many pieces to it, but the most important piece of the puzzle is making it fun!

Just Dance!

I happen to love to dance, maybe you do, too. Dancing is great exercise and a fun way for students to get the wiggles out. One of the first dances I teach students is the "Chicken Dance." Kids love it and so do I! We also have fun doing the Cupid Shuffle and the Cha Cha slide for a little "Old School" fun! When your class has been working hard and need a little fun, Just Dance!

Create Special Days

There are lots of fun days to celebrate if we pay attention! Did you know that September 19 is "Talk Like a Pirate Day?" Do a search and find out the dates of special days that you can have fun with your students in the classroom.

Celebrate

Celebrations for holidays and birthdays aren't the only time you can celebrate with your students. How about a celebration for end of testing? How about having a fun Game Day afternoon when students have successfully completed a unit in Math? I like the idea of celebrating with your class to reward them for a job well done! The key is making the celebration spontaneous. Example, *"You have all done such a great job finishing your History Hero Reports that I think it's time for a celebration. On Friday bring a treat and we will share our reports with each other and watch a movie I found about one of the Heros you learned about!"*

Reflect and Write

How will you create fun in your classroom?

Building Community with Parents

Once you win over your students, your parents will quickly get on board and become partners. This is often an area where teachers can become uncomfortable because often the first time they contact a parent is when a child is in trouble. Don't let this happen to you! Get to know your parents and do whatever you can to make connections. The letter home to parents is a great first step, but don't forget that phone calls are also very personal. Create a plan to help you get to know your parents and invite them to visit your classroom during the school day as soon as you feel comfortable. They will feel comforted when they see their children in the classroom setting and it will give them a picture of what their child's school day is like.

I am sure your school has many opportunities for parents to be included at school, but if it doesn't you might want to consider creating opportunities in your own classroom. Invite parents to visit and spend time with their children in class. When students have completed a project or units, invite parents to come see the work they have done, or watch their presentations and performances.

Parent Volunteers

Parents also like to volunteer in classrooms, but it is important to provide opportunities and structure their volunteer visits to make their visits useful. Working parents might be able to provide support by helping to organize class parties, make calls to invite parents to chaperone field trips, or make treats for the class to enjoy. Many parents do want to work in the classroom and in my experience this has been helpful if I planned for their visit and had jobs for them to do. Parents enjoy working at centers with students, reading to students, and playing games with students either one on one, or in small groups. It does take effort on your part to make sure the experience is meaningful for the parent, and actually helpful to you!

Plan for Volunteers to Support your Classroom	
What are volunteer jobs that would be helpful to me and my students?	
How will I schedule and plan for volunteers in my classroom?	
How will I inform parents about volunteer opportunities and organize their visits?	

Your Dream Community is Also for You!

You are the key to community in your classroom, your school, and outside of school. The community is just as much of a support to *you*, as it is for your students, parents, and colleagues. It is important to participate as much as you can in the life of the school. There are times when you need to work in your classroom over lunch, but it is important that you eat lunch together with your grade level team, as well! Building relationships with colleagues will provide you with support and friendship that will last throughout your teaching career and beyond. Attending school and community functions is also important because they show that you want to connect and be a part of the community. Your presence at events outside of the school day is more relaxed and you will make great connections with students, parents, and staff. Get involved as much as you can and the payoff will be that you will also be part of the "Dream" community. That community will provide you comfort and support as you grow and develop throughout your career.

Here I am with some of the Dream Teachers, I worked with in Malaysia. These ladies have fun working together and provide support to each other every day! They have created a Dream Community for themselves, and their students!

Make a Plan to Create Community in Your Classroom!

You have heard many ideas to create community and you have ideas of your own. Imagine what your Dream Classroom community will look like and feel like. How are you going to achieve your dream? Use the template below to jot down your ideas and list the steps you will take to create your classroom community. The payoff for your students and for you will be amazing as your class begins to live and work together in peace and harmony!

What will my Dream Classroom Community look like?	How will I create my Dream Classroom Community?	What steps will I take to develop my Dream Classroom Community?	What will I do to become a part of our School Community?

What Books, Games and Songs will I use to Create my Dream Classroom Community?		
Great Books for Class Meetings	**Fun Songs to Sing that have a positive message.**	**Fun games and Activities that encourage students to work together**

Creating a Community for a Lifetime

Creating a Community in your classroom will help you and your students have the best school year ever. Without a community the students and the teacher will feel isolated and unsupported. Creating a sense of community starting on the first day of school will help every student to have that strong sense of belonging that they need to be secure and successful at school. The community you begin on day one will strengthen and grow throughout the school year. When students feel like part of a community they will l learn how to support and care for each other. By creating a classroom community, you are teaching your students valuable skills that will last them a lifetime!

Tips from the Pros!

Question #1: What are some of your favorite Read-Aloud books that you read to students at the beginning of the school year and in class meetings?

Carole *The Dot* and *The Word Collector*, by Peter H. Reynolds. All of his books are great and have wonderful messages for children of all ages!

Jenny I agree! I love all of his (Peter H. Reynolds's) books and I use them at the beginning of the year and throughout the year during our Social Emotional Learning time. Another of my favorites is *The Name Jar*, by Yangsook Choi.

Susan Keven Henkes' books are good, "all about me" stories! (*Chrysanthemum, Chester's Way, Julius, the Baby of the World, Owen, Waiting, Wemberly Worried, Sheila Rae, the Brave, Kitten's First Full Moon, Lilly's Big Day.*)

Isabel *The Kissing Hand, Mrs. Bindergarten goes to Kindergarten,* and *David, No, David!*

Vickie The book *One* is awesome!

Ann Marie *The Big Orange Splot* is a favorite of mine. Great for talking about self, expressing individuality and respect of each other.

Question #2: How do you communicate with parents?

Gillian In the UAE we use Class DoJo and WhatsApp.

Isabel We use Seesaw for messaging back and forth. We also post pictures and videos of sweet things and reminders like, "Don't Forget It's Spirit Night Tonight!" We also send home a weekly class newsletter with academics and other classroom happenings. (We use paper, many of our parents don't have email.)

Jenny I send home a digital newsletter. We also use email and I have a class Twitter account related to my class and the school. Additionally, I have a private Class Instagram account to post pictures of class activities. To communicate individually to a parents I use email, text, and make a phone call! As much as possible I speak to parents in person as needed.

Chelsea Many of my students do not have technology at home so I send home a good old-fashioned newsletter!

Discussion Questions

1. Why is creating a "Classroom Community," so important? How will your community support student learning?
2. How will Class Meetings help to build your Dream Classroom community?
3. How will you greet students and start their day on a positive start the first day and every day?

4. How will you build a partnership with parents?
5. How will you use volunteers in your classroom?
6. Why are picture books a great way to teach children about feelings, respect, and other important topics related to their Social-Emotional development? What are the titles of some books that you plan to use in your classroom?

> **Notes to Trainers and Mentors**
>
> Creating a community begins with the teachers in your school. How are you building community and creating a family feel between staff members? Think of ways you can develop a feeling of community in your school by creating special opportunities to work together on fun projects and activities with each other, the students, and the community. Brainstorm ideas with your staff to discover ways that you can bring staff together and have fun!
>
> Consider how your school uses volunteers and work together with the teachers to create a school-wide plan. There are many ways that parents and community members can support teachers and students, but there needs to be a plan in place to make that happen. Volunteers feel useful when they are assigned meaningful jobs in the school that match their skillset. Of course, celebrating the work that volunteers do across the school is also important!

Self Assessment

Check the boxes that match you!

I have communicated with parents to introduce myself and invite them to visit our classroom.	
I send a newsletter home to parents to keep them informed.	
I have a variety of opportunities planned for parents to volunteer in my classroom.	
I have scheduled times for Class Meetings to support students' social and emotional development.	
My students are starting to work together as a team and support each other.	
I have fun with my students through a variety of activities throughout the week.	
I am working together with my own team to build a supportive community.	

My Next Steps

Develop Your Dream Classroom Routines

Dream Classrooms run smoothly with careful planning to create routines and procedures and high expectations for students. When children know how to move about the classroom safely, access resources and work together in learning space they will feel comfortable and safe. Classroom expectations and routines that are consistently implemented will encourage positive student behavior and good work habits. In this chapter you will create a plan for your classroom so students can enjoy learning together in their Dream Classroom.

Planning Routines for your Dream Classroom

A Dream Classroom needs carefully thought out and planned routines and procedures to ensure that children know the "What, When, Where, Why and Hows" of moving around and using resources in their classroom. Once students feel confident to follow the routines independently they will enjoy learning in a happy and safe environment. Children thrive on structure and routines provide a safety net for young learners. It is your job as a Dream Teacher to carefully think through the routines before students come into your classroom and design a plan to teach and implement the routines to your students. Time spent at the start of the school year pays off in short order, but keep in mind that students need review after weekends and breaks. Build time into the "first day back" after a long weekend or holiday recess to review processes and expectations. Avoid assuming that once students know, they should always know. Young minds forget, and the game plan is different at home and other locations. The teacher's efforts to remain consistent, though it's sometimes challenging and exhausting, are vital to success.

Morning Entry

Let's begin with classroom entry. Greeting students at the door is one of the most powerful ways to get your students' day off to a positive start. Share a smile, a high five, or whatever fits your personality and let your students know you are happy to see them. Too many of the students we support are waking themselves up in the morning, getting ready for school on their own, and don't connect with a caring adult before leaving for school. Creating that "welcome" at the start of the day is a critical step towards establishing a caring culture.

Once students enter the classroom where will they store their belongings? Lockers? Cubbies? Hooks? Wherever there is space in your classroom you need to plan where you want students to store their coats, bags, and whatever else they bring to school. So think about it. Can you identify their space with students' names? Once they put away their belongings do you want them to go to their seat? Is there a special spot for students to put their homework? What will they do once they get to their seats? Read a book? Morning work? You need to think about what you want your *Dream Classroom* to look like during morning entry and throughout the day and begin to establish important routines on the first day of school.

In the space below brainstorm your ideas for routines and procedures for morning entry and throughout the day.

Starting the Day in a Positive Way!

So now your students are all in the classroom, they are seated and doing their morning work. The school announcements and pledge are completed and you are ready to begin your students' day of learning. So how will you do that? One big mistake that so many teachers make is they immediately begin the lessons. "Ok, kids, get out your Math books and turn to page 31." Starting your day this way is a recipe for disaster! Why? Because students need to know what their day is going to look like.

Routines and Procedures to Start the Year		
Activity	**Routines** *What you expect*	**Procedures** *How it is done*
Morning Entry Where do students put their belongings and homework? What other expectations do you have for morning entry?		
Morning "Start Now" What are the expectations for morning work? (Read, Journal Entry, Math Review) (This is what students do while waiting for everyone to arrive and get settled.)		
Accessing Resources Will you have supplies on tables? Is there a supply center? Do students keep their own supplies in their desks?		
Walking in the Hallways Will students line up inside your classroom door in ABC order? What are your expectations for walking with your class outside of the classroom?		
Bathroom Breaks Will you give group breaks? Do students use a pass when they need to go? Where is the pass and how do they get it?		
Whole Group Carpet Time How will students move from their desks or tables, to the carpet? What are your expectations for sitting together on the carpet?		
Work and Center Time What will work time look like in your classroom? Will students always be at their desks? How much talking is acceptable? What will you be doing? Conferencing? Small groups? What do students do if they finish?		

I have previously covered the importance of gathering your students together in a community to start your day. I can't stress it enough! Start the day with greeting the students and checking in with them to see how they are doing. Give students an opportunity to share or ask questions. Go over the day's schedule that you have posted on the board. Let them know about any special programs, assemblies, or activities that they will be doing that day. Letting students know the plan for the day will give them time to process and prepare for the expectations you have for them for the day.

It is also important to take time in the morning to have a class meeting. Some teachers tell me they don't have time every day. Please, don't let the pressure of getting through chapters in the book, teaching each standard and testing keep you from focusing on the social-emotional needs of your students. Pushing the curriculum will not help them to learn better or faster! Spending time to set the stage for learning is the most valuable piece of the learning puzzle. Start every day as a community and set children up for learning. Plan time for a class meeting at least two to three times a week. This is the time when you can make connections with your students, give them time to share their thoughts and discuss issues that may be on their minds. Building relationships with your students and between your students is the first step to creating your *Dream Classroom* where all students feel safe, accepted, and loved!

Check out the book *Have You Filled Your Bucket Today? The Key to Being Happy* by Carol McCloud and Caryn Butzke. Do some "Bucket Filling" at your next class meeting!

Setting Guidelines, "Rules or Expectations"

Every classroom and school in the world has rules. Rules are important because they keep us safe. But how many rules do we need? And what happens if a rule is broken? These are issues that every teacher needs to consider before students come into their classrooms. And what should you call them? The word, "RULES," can have a negative connotation because that word is usually connected with consequences. Whatever you call them I recommend you don't have too many. In my children's book, *My Grandma's Crazy!*, Grandma has two rules.

How We Want our Class to be

Try starting on the first day of school with a class discussion and ask students to think how they want their class to be. You will find out quickly that the students want the same thing that you want! Students want to be in a classroom where everyone is respected. The word "Respect" is key to helping your students design their own classroom expectations. When you involve students in setting up the expectations for classroom behavior they will buy into the program and work together to create a classroom environment where everyone feels safe, respected, and happy! It seems to work best when it comes from them, so give it a try. Your conversation with students may go something like this.

THINK/PAIR/SHARE

"Today is the first day of school and we are going to work together to identify important standards we can all follow so that we can be happy and learn together in our classroom. Think about how you want our class to be. When I give the signal share your ideas with a partner. I will listen to your conversations and together we will create a chart to show our thoughts."

(Listen to children's discussions to report back and ask for new ideas to create a chart similar to the one below.)

Your chart may look something like this:

How we want our class to be:
Fun
Happy
Everyone should be nice
No yelling out
No hitting or shoving
No bullying
We should do our work
We should help each other.

Once your chart is completed ask students to group their ideas together. These can now become the class expectations. *"I will treat others the way I want to be treated,"* or *"I will show respect to my classmates, my teachers, and my classroom environment,"* are just two examples you may want to try.

Post the agreed upon expectations and review them with your class every morning.

> **Class Expectations:**
>
> We will treat each other with respect.
>
> We will respect our classroom and school environment.
>
> We will follow routines and procedures.

I recommend you read a wonderful story to your students that explains the concept of treating others the way you want to be treated called *The Golden Rule* by Irene Cooper.

Teaching the Routines

Together your class has established standards to live by and important expectations for how to treat each other with respect. How will you actually teach students to follow these expectations and learn all of the routines and procedures that you have planned? Well I would like to tell you that you can tell the students the important routines and they will do it, but unfortunately that wouldn't really be the truth! Routines and procedures have to be taught, modeled, and practiced many times before they become automatic. This takes time at the start of the school year and for some classes it will take the first month of school, but some classes may even take longer. Routines must be implemented starting on day one and the expectations for these routines must be reinforced throughout the school year. A Dream Teacher will review these expectations, routines, and procedures for the class after a long weekend, a holiday, and any other time the class needs a reminder!

So what does this look like? Let me share with you an experience I had with a boys' school in Abu Dhabi. I was the school advisor and arrived four weeks into the school year. My assignment was to support the English teachers in grades 1–3. I visited classrooms and was amazed and a little shocked at what I saw. In grade 1 boys were on the tables, under the tables, running around the room and the teachers were completely frazzled.

Our first order of business was to begin teaching the boys important routines. Even though we spoke English, and they spoke Arabic, I was sure we could get our expectations across to them through modeling and practicing the routines. After all, they stood in perfect lines every day for morning assembly and followed the directions of the Arabic speaking staff. They just needed to get to know the expectations of their English teachers.

The teachers and I all agreed that we would teach the boys to walk in a line to their classroom door, line up along the wall, and go into their classroom to their seats in an orderly manner. It took all of us showing the boys, modeling, and practicing over and over until they understood. Teachers put their names on the tables in English and we allowed four boys into the classroom at a time. We showed them where to sit, and how to pull out the chair quietly and be seated. This took time, as you can imagine. We had to practice this routine every day and we were consistent with our expectations. Some classes got into the routine quickly, and other classes took several weeks before they could follow the new routines.

Routines and Procedures at the End of the Day!

Your day will fly by and before you know it's dismissal time. Don't let your day end with students flying out of the room and you left with the mess of the day! Plan your dismissal and train your students for leaving the classroom as carefully as you planned for them to arrive! Make sure you have a visible clock and it is showing the correct time! One of your student's jobs could be the class timekeeper! You could also set a timer to give you and the class a signal that it is time to close the day. Students should be responsible for putting resources away, cleaning the room, straightening up their desks, and getting their homework into their backpacks. This takes time and training!

I recommend that you have time to end the class with a short class meeting. Give students a review and wrap up of their day, compliments, and of course, homework assignments. Students also like to review their day. A quick assessment of their feelings about the day could be a Thumbs Up/Thumbs Sideways/Thumbs Down. Exit tickets are also a great way to get kids out of the door by writing something they learned that day. And just like you greeted your students in the morning, be sure to give them a warm send off in the afternoon! *Enjoy the rest of the day. I can't wait to see you again tomorrow.* Once a teacher knows his/her students better, make it personal—such as *I bet Milo (pet) can't wait for you to get home. I hope your grandma feels better today. I can't wait to hear what happens next in that book you're reading at home.* It's the personal touch and that strong connection with their teacher that helps students to feel that strong sense of belonging at school.

Use the planning chart below to plan your class dismissal!

How much time will my class need for dismissal?	
What do I expect students to do to prepare for dismissal?	
What will my role be as my class prepares for dismissal?	
How will my class line up and leave the classroom?	

Helping your Students to Make Good Choices!

Your routines and procedures are in place. Students are learning these routines and meeting the class expectations most of the time! However, you have noticed that there are some students that are not always making good choices. Making good choices is a life skill and your job as a teacher is to help them to be successful and feel good about themselves. There are many theories, approaches, books, experts, and schools of thought about discipline. Discipline is not a list of rules and consequences. Discipline is not a system of, "You do THIS, and you get THAT!" Discipline means, "To Teach," and that is the job that you will do every day as you teach children to make good decisions. This may be the most important job you will have with some of your neediest students!

Consequences Vs Problem Solving

Our goal as a teacher is to help our students to make good choices. When children make a bad choice they never feel good about it. Giving a student a consequence is punishment, but it doesn't really help children to learn how to make a better choice next time. When children are given a consequence, but there is no problem solving done to fix the problem, they can become angry and resentful. Problem solving takes time, but it is important time spent. Talking to a student and asking them to describe the problem is the first step. Once a student admits they have made a bad choice and start showing remorse the process has started. When children feel bad for what they have done you are part way there. The next step is to help the student to find a way to make things right. Restitution can mean writing a sorry note, talking to a student you have offended and saying sorry and cleaning up the mess, in this way a child will learn from their mistakes. You may even want to give a student a problem-solving sheet to get the process started! Finally, if you do give a student a consequence it should ALWAYS tie to the issue. Many times, our students don't have a clue what the right choices are because no one has ever shared that with them. Take the time to problem solve and talk to a child to help them to recognize and make good choices every day!

Problem Solving Sheet	
What is the problem?	
Describe what happened.	
How do you feel?	
How do the other student/students feel?	
How can you solve the problem and make things right?	

Some Children Need More

In my experience there are usually at least one or two students who need more of my attention and take more of my time than the others. When you have a student who has more challenging behavior it is important for you to have some extra tools in your tool kit. There is never a "one size fits all" answer to discipline. What works magic for one student, may be a disaster for another. If you have a student that is having difficulty here are some suggestions for you to try.

Time-Outs

Sometimes a student isn't ready to resolve a problem and needs time away from the other students. A time-out area in your classroom can give students a quiet place to reflect, have a good cry, and even begin to problem solve. A time out spot may also be needed because you don't have time to help solve the problem at that moment. I have heard of so many great ideas for a time-out spot. Two of my favorites are teachers who send their student to a far away vacation spot. Vickie created a spot in the back of her classroom and she called it "Australia." Australia is far away and it was quiet. This was a good place to have a little "get away." Karen sent her students to "Hawaii." She created a relaxing retreat with posters and brochures that she collected from local travel agencies. If a child was having a problem, looking stressed, or having an issue she would say to them, "I think you may need to take a trip to Hawaii. Go take a break and when you feel better you can come back and join the class." Karen said this worked so well that she rarely had to send any of her students out of the classroom.

Teacher Buddy

It is a good idea to have a Teacher Buddy in a classroom next to yours. Sometimes a student needs a time-out from the classroom. If you have a colleague that is willing to work with one of your students to provide respite from your classroom this can be an excellent way to give a child that is struggling a change of scenery. A Teacher Buddy is never the disciplinarian. When a student walks into their classroom they are to be calmly greeted and directed to their time-out space. When a student has a time-out in their own classroom, or a Teacher Buddy's classroom they will still be exposed to grade level curriculum and lessons. Whether a student is in time-out in your classroom, or your colleague's, it is important that they return to join the class after 5–10 minutes.

Contact a Parent

Hopefully you have been building your relationship with parents and the first call you make is not when they child has misbehaved or is in trouble. You should always speak to a parent in person when you have concerns. Don't ever put negative news in a text or email. Parents will hear in your voice that you are concerned and that you care. Giving parents bad news is never easy, but when you approach it with concern you will find that parents are your best resource. Starting a conversation with, "Mrs. Jones, I'm calling because I need your help with Johnny's behavior in the classroom" will get more positive results than, "Mrs. Jones, I'm calling because Johnny had a bad day and I sent him to the office!" It is often a good idea to think through what you are going to say and even write it down before you make that call! It is also important to have some ideas of what you would like that parent to do to provide support. (Could you talk to him tonight, come visit class tomorrow, give consequences at home, sign a daily check sheet, etc.) And don't forget to ask parents for suggestions because they know their child better than anyone!

Behavior Contracts, Charts, and Positive Motivation!

We want children to make good decisions, However, children are all different and sometimes they need a little help. A behavior plan should be simple and straightforward. It will work best if the parents are on board with you and support the plan at home, just like you do at school. A behavior plan only works if the adults are consistent. Any inconsistency on the adult end will negate any positive progress that has been made. Identify one behavior that you want the child to improve. Create a simple behavior check sheet that students will carry home every day. It is important that you check it daily, confer with the student about the success of the day, or improvements needed the next day. A good day is often rewarded with a heart, a star, or a sticker. Sometimes a student will respond well to earning stickers to receive a larger reward that ideally comes from parents. When you create a check sheet be sure to include two behaviors that you know the child will succeed in and only one that needs improvement! This ensures that a child gets at least two positive strokes on their chart each day.

Here is an example:

_____'s Behavior Check List

Teacher Signature _____

Parent Signature _____

Child's Signature _____

Comments _____

Directions: Teacher will keep the check list and record progress at the end of each day with the student. The Sheet will go home on Friday to parents.

Date	Monday	Tuesday	Wednesday	Thursday	Friday
I kept my hands to myself.					
I was kind to my classmates.					
I completed my work.					

Forgive and Forget!

Students want to be good. I often tell parents, "She/He, would be good, if she could! She wants to please you, and make you happy!" I worked together with parents, colleagues, or on my own, to explore every angle to determine the source of a child's anger, or issues. I spent time getting to know that child, making him or her my assistant, inviting them to spend time with me during lunch or before school. In short, I did everything I could think of to help the student to make good choices, to do their best work, and to be happy in school.

When I became a principal I always had a round table where children could come to finish work, or have a breather from the classroom. I had a "Thinking" chair where students could process an issue they were having and come up with solutions. Once they were done "Thinking," we would have a talk and come up with a plan to help them to be successful when they returned to the class. When you get this close to a student there are times when you will feel betrayed because they slipped up, or got in trouble, again! These are times when you need to remember they are a child. Once the storm is over, forgive them, forget it, give them a hug and move on!

Follow Your heart!

I will close this chapter with stories from Dream Teachers that have made a difference in the lives of children. The first story is from Gillian. Gillian is an experienced American teacher who moved to Abu Dhabi to teach. Her first assignment was in a boys' school with a class of active first graders. While language was a barrier she was able to connect and share her heart with her boys starting the first day. Gillian introduced and taught important class routines and the boys responded. She read to the boys, taught them American songs and even shared with them her favorite American pop music! The class quickly responded and teaching and learning came together quickly. Gillian shared with me one of her early experiences with the boys that showed me that discipline often comes down to following your heart!

Part way through one particularly rough morning Gillian noticed that the boys were off and acting out. She stopped teaching and brought all the boys into a circle into the middle of the room. They were expecting to be in big trouble. Gillian went around the circle to each little boy and touched them on their shoulder. She told each boy, *"You're a good boy, you're a good boy, you're a good boy,"* until she made it all around the circle. She softly told them that she loved them and they were all good boys. To make sure they understood she taught them each to say, *"I'm a good boy"* and point to themselves. The second time she went around the circle the boys repeated *"I'm a good boy, I'm a good boy, I'm a good boy."* She gave them each a hug and they continued their day. She told me that now she starts every day by reminding them that they are all *"Good Boys!"*

Ms. Gillian with her boys ready to celebrate National Day!

I asked my Dream Teachers if they would share a personal story of a time they made a difference in one of their students' lives. Here are some of their responses!

Dawn Marie "There were twin boys in our middle school, one on each 8th grade team. The young man on our team would sometimes get so angry that he just couldn't contain himself. If my room was empty and he was having trouble staying calm, he would go in my room and sit on the floor and rock or growl or cry. Whatever he needed. I would keep checking on him or just sit by him until he was able to go to class again. There was a time I was trying to get him to go on a field trip to Lake Michigan with his team of 8th graders, but he kept coming up with reasons that he couldn't go. I tried talking to his mom about helping him to go. He still didn't go the day of the trip. About six weeks later, he and his twin left our school and moved out of the county with family. About five years later, we had a staff meeting before school started and it was these two young men. They had both just graduated from high school. They came to tell us what an impact their 8th grade teachers had on their lives. They told us about how their families had drugs in the home and they had been encouraged to begin selling drugs. They moved because they were able to get out of their home and go live with other family members. My young man began crying. This big 6'3" young man . . . crying and saying 'Thank you Mrs. Kahler. You never gave up on me and you cared about me.' He was crying uncontrollably. The entire staff was silent and crying. I just had to run to the front of the room and hug him. I didn't want him to feel embarrassed because he was a grown man crying in front of an audience of teachers. He couldn't get any more words out, but he said so much. I am such a blessed teacher to have experienced such a moment."

Claudia "My best example was a boy with poor social skills and high functioning Autism. He lived two miles down the road from me. I had him 'earn' coming over and shooting hoops with me and my son, using a behavior plan. He not only learned to trust me, he would ride his bike by and say hi to me whenever I jogged by his house. He needed a friend. I also partnered my nicest boys with him and coached them in ways to include him. He had success in my class!"

Lynne "When I was a deputy principal in a high school (years 7 to 12, Australia) I got to know many students and their family backgrounds especially those with behavioural issues. I knew a new year 7 boy was coming to the school from a difficult background where the mother had a history of drug abuse, but she did her best. This boy was violent in the community and primary school but he was also bright and interested in learning. I established a good relationship with him early on and offered to assist with any homework/assignments. He would be a regular visitor to my office. I gave him TIME and encouragement. I also fed back to his class teachers about him and his desire to learn. Sure he had discipline referrals which we worked through. He knew I had high expectations and believed he could achieve. He also worked with the other Deputy. We encouraged him and provided a safe place to resolve issues. We encouraged him to run for a school leadership position when he was in year 11. This included giving a speech to the cohort. His speech went through several drafts, was honest about his early unacceptable behaviour both at school and in the community. It was a very proud moment when he was elected vice captain of the school. Summing up I would say the important points are: establish a supportive, trusting relationship; forgive outbursts and discuss how to move forward (avoid judgment); school discipline policies need to be followed including suspension but if a student knows that you really care about them, you can enforce discipline and then get back on track."

You can be the Teacher that makes the difference!

Developing your classroom environment, putting into place your routines, procedures, and expectations, and creating a team or a family in your classroom, is the most important piece of the Dream Classroom puzzle that you are putting together. But don't forget that YOU are the key to success with every child in your care. We don't know where students have been, we don't know what they face when they go home, and we don't know what it is like to walk in their shoes. But one thing we do know is that we may be the one person in that child's life that will take the time to listen and care enough to do whatever it takes to help that child to be successful in school and happy in life. Be kind, listen, and show your students that you care. Sometimes we don't know the impact we have had on our students until years later, but you just may be the one teacher that will make a difference in the life of a child!

Tips from the Pros!

Question #1: What Behavior Management Plan do you use in your classroom?

Erinn As a sub, mine is a bit different. I follow what the teachers use, but I also introduce myself at the beginning of the day as Ms. Egg. I tell the class that at the end of the day, I will pick one student who exemplified Good Egg behavior. I try to tie this into IB profiles of outstanding citizenship. At the end of the day, room cleaned, I give out a plastic "Easter" egg with a small prize—tattoo, cheap plastic toy, etc. I keep a record of each class and the student who received the Egg. That way I don't repeat in the same school year and I make sure boys and girls are fairly recognized. I let the entire class know WHY the child received the Egg and then encourage them to applaud for their classmate. I have been doing this for three years (all elementary) and the kids are very aware of the Eggs I carry.

Chelsea Jo PAWS
Prepare daily
Accept responsibility
Work hard
Show respect

Everyone starts out on five! Mistakes happen but more than once in a while needs a friendly reminder. Paw moves down. The goal is to have the maximum amount of points needed at the end of the month to attend the classroom PAWS party to celebrate our great behavior.

Question #2: How do you get your class's attention?

Claudia Two quick loud claps. No one else is allowed to do it in class, so they know it's me "calling to all." For attention when I need them to be quiet, I just raise my hand with two fingers up.

Hannah I say "Texas, Texas!" And they reply "Yee-haw!" This is to get everyone quiet. It's a cheer from college.

Anne-Marie I used "Give Me Five" from day one . . . Love it still!

Question #3: How do you handle a student with disruptive, or repeated, misbehavior?

Karen

- Arrange a special mentor for a child with high needs. Identify a building adult who connects well with the student, and ask him or her to work with you to design a connection with the student. I had several 6th and 7th graders that I did this with, and the special mentor for one was the middle school custodian (who was a super cool guy), and the other was a football coach. The key is to "find a fit." It needs to be someone who is willing and able to make a connection. It could be a former teacher, the nurse, the librarian, a music teacher, etc. It could be a parent volunteer. Be creative.

- Eat lunch with a high needs student – set up a system to *earn this*. Back in the day, I actually ordered McDonalds for us to eat together, and the food was donated by that McDonalds because I made the effort to meet with the manager and explain my plan. It was a special bonding time that revolved around a positive social conversation. Years back, you could get a permission slip from the parent, and take the student in your own car. Not sure that this is recommended any more—what a shame. It was a powerful and memorable treat for both of us.

- Meet privately with high needs students to determine ways that they can "help" in the classroom. Are they a perfect buddy for another student? Are they excited to help with tasks such as sweeping or organizing a particular area of the room? I had a student who loved to accompany the custodian at the end of the day for 15 minutes – picking up hallway pencils, pushing the mop, etc. It wasn't about being fancy. It was about feeling special, and having a purpose.

Chelsea Create a "Safe Zone" in the classroom where particular students can go to write, color, and decompress.

Claudia Our school used Responsible Thinking Classroom. If a student disrupts the learning process they get a warning the first time. The second time they get a time out in the classroom. The third time they go out of the classroom to work with a counselor to write a plan. They bring the plan back to the class and when the teacher is free to talk to them about the plan they are allowed to return to the group. This system worked well for most students.

Discussion Questions

1. How does your classroom environment, routines and procedures and personal touch help to motivate students to do their very best in school?
2. What is your biggest challenge related to student behavior? What strategies can you put into place to address this challenge?
3. Describe the difference between consequences and Problem Solving? Is there ever a time when a consequence is warranted? Describe a time that you solved a problem with a student and they started to make better choices.
4. Why is there no "One Size Fits All" approach that works for all of your students? Give an example of a time you might use a different approach with a student.
5. Which personal story from a teacher or "Tip from the Pros" stood out to you? Why?

Notes to Trainers and Mentors

Behavior management is often the area where teachers struggle most. Spend time with your group going over behavior policies at your school and acquaint them with resources that may be available to them if they have students who need additional support.

Self Assessment

Check the boxes that match you!

I have planned procedures for morning entry to the classroom.	
I am teaching and modeling my expectations for routines and procedures to my students.	
I am consistent with my expectations.	
I am teaching students how to respect each other through lessons and class meetings.	
I treat all children with respect and show them that I care for them.	
I work through conflict with my class and students through conflict resolution, not punishment.	
I am recognizing the special needs of some of my students and have developed a plan so they can be successful in my class.	

My Next Steps

Plan Your Dream Classroom Lessons

Great lessons are planned and they don't happen by accident. Planning for learning is essential to good classroom instruction. The heart of your Dream Classroom will be the lessons that you teach. This chapter will focus on designing great lessons that meet the needs of every child in your classroom!

Be Smart—Plan Smart!

There is no magic to great lessons. Sometimes it looks like magic when you watch a skilled teacher deliver a great lesson, but I promise you, a lot of thought and planning went into it. Dream Teachers plan their lessons and purposely choose high impact teaching strategies, compelling resources, and student activities that will ignite student learning. It's no accident that a great teacher, gets great results. When you are planning a lesson for your students this is your chance to be creative. Who knows your class better than you? Whatever standard you teach, you can choose the teaching strategies, resources, and activities that will meet the needs of every student.

Here is what we will cover in this chapter to get you well on your way to planning your Dream Classroom lessons!

- **Learning Standards**—Learn why standards are important, how to read them, and how to plan lessons to teach them.

- **Teaching Strategies**—High Impact Teaching strategies will be identified for you to choose from that will be great additions to your learning tool-kit.
- **Student Activities**—A variety of engaging student activities will be defined to give students more opportunities to read, write, create, and show what they know!
- **Integrating Literacy Across the Curriculum**—Get ideas to create a classroom environment that is rich in print and learn literacy strategies to support reading and writing across content areas.
- **Writing a Lesson**—You will learn to write a targeted lesson plan with a clear beginning, middle, and end that will incorporate Gradual Release into every lesson. (I do, We do, You do!)

Steps to Good Planning

Identify the Learning Standard

When I first started teaching we had no standards. I remember entering my first 5th grade classroom before school started and going down the hall to ask a teacher what we should teach. She pretty much said, "use the reading and Math books. We have some old Health books and a few Science books, but no Social Studies books." Ok—that was pretty wide open and didn't give me a lot to go on. I remember those first years of teaching fondly and because I was a pretty good teacher, I made it work. I followed the reading program and used the Math books. We went to the library frequently and my students did research and projects related to Science and Social Studies. I basically tried to remember what *I* learned in school and passed that on to my students. I taught my students how to write stories, poems, and reports. They researched countries of South America and created projects and presentations. We had silent reading every day after lunch, went on walking field trips to the University, local museums, and to the Public Library. I was pretty sure students were learning but I had no official assessments to prove that. My students took a state test and the Iowa Test of Basic Skills, but neither were aligned to what we were teaching. We gave grades and if their report card was good we figured they learned. I do remember that my students worked hard and we had fun learning together.

Today School Districts around the world have set Learning Standards. In the United States, we have Common Core Standards that are set across the nation to provide common standards for students no matter what state they live in. Now districts have a clear picture of what students should be taught to prepare students for college and careers. Lucky you! You have standards that have been set for each subject and grade level that takes the "Guess Work" out of teaching. These standards are your road map to teaching and learning!

Knowing the standards for your subject and grade is vital to planning great lessons. The first step is to access the learning standards and become familiar with them before you begin planning. Learning Standards are set for each grade level and the expectation is that all children will meet those standards. Standards are repeated each year, but they increase in rigor and are applied at higher levels, as students move up through the grades. This makes it even more important that your students master grade level standards to help them to be successful the following school year.

Here is an example:

Reading Literature

*RL.K.9—**With prompting** and support **compare and contrast** the adventures and experiences of characters in familiar stories.*

*RL.4.9—**Compare and Contrast** the treatment of similar themes and topics (e.g. opposition of good and evil) and patterns of events in stories, myths, and and traditional literature from different cultures.*

Reflect and Write

How do the standards change from Kindergarten to 4th grade? How does the rigor increase?

As you become familiar with standards I encourage you to look at the same standard you are teaching to see how it is applied in the grades above and below your grade level. It will give you an idea of what students have been taught and where they will be expected to go with it in the future. Knowing the standard will help you to target your lessons to the specific objective your students will need to learn.

How Do You Read a Standard?

To understand a standard read it carefully to pinpoint what students need to know and what they are expected to do. Within the standard highlight the skill being taught, which begins with an action verb. *Compare and Contrast, Analyze, Describe, Determine,* are some examples. Once you have established the skill students are expected to learn, read the standard to establish how it should be applied.

Take a look at this second grade Math Standard as an example:

Mathematics—Operations and Algebraic Thinking

2.0A.A.1—Use addition and subtraction within 100 to solve one and two step word problems involving situations of adding to, taking from, putting together, taking apart, and comparing with unknowns in all positions. E.g. by using drawings and equations with a symbol for the unknown number to represent the problem.

There is a lot to this standard. Students will be expected to apply addition and subtraction up to 100 to solve one and two step word problems. They will also be expected to use a symbol for an unknown number to represent the problem. As you prepare this lesson you may want to ask yourself a couple questions:

- Can my students add and subtract single and double digit numbers up to 100?
- Do my students understand the Academic Vocabulary listed in the standard?
- Do my students know the symbols for equations in number problems?
- How will I assess my students before, during, and after the lesson?

Becoming familiar with the standards you are teaching will help you to plan lessons that are targeted to the specific needs of your students. Being aware of the skills students need to know will help you to provide the right scaffolding and support for students to be successful.

Reflect and Write

What would be a good "first step" to approaching this standard with your students before they begin writing a word problem with a symbol?

Determine the Teaching Strategy

Once you have determined the standard you are going to teach you will start to think about how you are going to teach it. Choosing the right teaching strategy is the next step in planning a great lesson. It is important to choose teaching strategies that have high impact and will meet the needs of all of the students in your class. Choosing strategies that include best practices in teaching and learning is vital to student success. One of the top experts in the world on this topic is John Hattie. He has analyzed over 500,000 studies related to student achievement and identified the teaching strategies that have the highest impact on student learning. Some of these strategies are listed below for you to consider as you plan your lessons. To learn more High Impact Strategies, I recommend the book *High Impact Strategies for Teachers* (John Hattie—Visible Learning, 2009).

1. **Direct Instruction**—A targeted lesson focused on a clear learning objective and success criteria.
2. **Note Taking and Other Study Skills**—Specific note taking and study skills strategies are taught and applied routinely throughout lessons.
3. **Spaced Practice**—New skills are best learned if they are introduced and returned to at various times to give students time to process and acquire the new skill.

4. **Feedback**—Providing feedback through coaching conversations with the teacher and with peers is one of the most valuable learning tools.
5. **Teaching Metacognitive Skills**—Metacognition is "Thinking about Thinking." Metacognitive skills include strategies for learning. This includes study skills, and self-instruction and self-assessment strategies.
6. **Teaching Problem Solving Skills**—Teaching students steps to problem solving and providing them with a process to solve problems is a valuable learning tool.
7. **Repeated Reading Programs**—practicing meaningful short passages of reading to gain fluency.
8. **Vocabulary Instruction**—Teaching vocabulary improves reading comprehension
9. **Concept Mapping**—Concept mapping is an important tool for brainstorming and creating new ideas. It is also a great tool for note taking.
10. **Worked Examples**—Students need to know what success looks like. A worked example is a chart, a picture, a drawing, or any other examples of the learning outcome to guide them through the learning process.

Reflect and Write

What teaching strategies are new to you? What new strategies would you like to try?

Choose the Student Activity

Say "NO" to worksheets!
Worksheets are the lowest level of student learning. Assigning worksheets and packets should be avoided. This includes word search puzzles, fill in the blank and multiple choice questions, and a full page of math problems to solve. The only worksheets that are really valuable are blank graphic organizers. If you think still want to give a worksheet to your students, ask yourself these questions:

1. Is this worksheet the best way for students to apply their knowledge and skills?
2. Is the worksheet a valuable use of my students' time?
3. Is there an alternative to this worksheet that would be a more motivating and valuable tool for my students to apply their learning?

If you still want to use a worksheet after considering these questions, consider sending it home with students for homework. Parents can assist students at home if there is a worksheet with directions. Read the variety of alternatives to worksheets in the following section. See if you can't find something that is more engaging and valuable for students to practice their skills and show their learning. I am sure you will enjoy the alternatives to worksheets as much as your students will.

Alternatives to Worksheets

Blank Books and Journals
Students benefit from having their own blank book for each subject to record their learning and apply their reading and writing skills. Students can take notes for each subject, record important vocabulary, written reflections, graphic organizers, charts, drawings, math facts and equations, and much more in their notebooks. The notebook becomes a chronological record of their learning for each subject. Students will see for themselves as their writing improves, and the notebook will become a treasured resource for unit projects and tests. Students will take ownership and pride in their learning journals and they will also become one of your most valuable tools for formative assessments.

Students take pride in their work when they write in their own Learning Journal.

Plan Your Dream Classroom Lessons ◆ 83

Mini Book

When you begin a new topic of study in class students will enjoy creating their own mini book, about that topic. The first day of the unit is a great time to begin a mini book as students design their own covers with a title and picture. The book is simple, construction paper for a cover with blank copy paper, stapled together! Students can record their notes, vocabulary, and keep their own research on the topic in their mini book. At the end of the unit the mini book will be filled with information, facts, and students' own questions and research about the topic.

Kindergarten students in Malaysia created their own mini books to celebrate their country!

Flip Books

Flip books are a fun and easy way for students to record vocabulary, Math facts, important information to learn, cause and effect, and a variety of important skills students are learning. Use construction paper and fold it in half. The front of the fold shows the term or idea, when you flip it up it shows the definition or explanation. Cut strips into the front page and students can list vocabulary words with the definition and picture showing when you flip it up. Students love to make flip books and they can write and draw their ideas to clarify their understanding.

Students enjoy sharing their flip books with each other!

Tri-folds

Tri-folds are another easy way to use construction paper for students to show their learning. Fold the paper into thirds for students to show the beginning/middle/end of a story. Or fold the paper in thirds to show the past/present/future of an event, technology, or their own life. Again, students can be creative, they can write and draw the information they want to share.

Graphic Organizers

There are many great graphic organizers to use with students to help them to clarify and record their thinking. I recommend that you choose four to five graphic organizers that you like and teach your students how to use them. Using a Venn diagram to compare and contrast is one example of a common graphic organizer that works for a variety of lessons. Here are samples of graphic organizers that you may want to try!

K-W-L Charts

Starting a new unit by creating an interactive K-W-L chart is an excellent way to get students to begin thinking about a topic. The chart builds and grows throughout the unit as students learn more about a topic and discover answers to their questions.

Here is an example of a K-W-L chart.

K (What do you Know about the topic?)	W (What do you Want to know about the topic?)	L (What did you Learn about the topic?)

Story Maps

Story Maps are a great way to record the important parts of a story. They can also be adapted to the standard you are teaching that is connected with the story. Story maps can be done together with the students following the story as an interactive charting activity.

Interactive charting engages students as they create their own story map. This story map then becomes a model for them as they read stories and create their own!

Learning Mats

Learning mats are an interactive charting strategy to use during Guided Reading groups. Students take ownership to their learning mat as they add their own predictions to stories, jot down unfamiliar vocabulary, and work together as a group to create a story map or graphic organizer that matches the standard they are learning. The learning mat sets the stage for learning on Monday and builds throughout the week as students finish the story and master the learning standard. The learning mat then becomes a record of what the group has accomplished!

A learning mat provides a focus for learning during small group instruction.

A learning mat can support your instruction and keep you and your group on target throughout a small group lesson. Jot your objectives or standards right on the mat to keep you focused throughout the lesson. Place the mats for each small group on top of one another to roll for easy storage so they will be ready to use the next day. Use the mat from the previous day to review what was learned in order to move forward with the new day's activity. Consider asking students to partner up on the last day of a Guided Reading text to summarize learning using cues from the learning mat. As a careful listener, this is your "Check for Understanding!"

Charting

There is no better way to build your print environment with you students than interactive charting. I have mentioned charting before and I will mention it again because it is so powerful. When you create a learning chart with students and hang it up you have a visual reminder of the important learning that is happening in the classroom. Charting is a great learning tool in every subject. As a classroom coach I love walking into a classroom to see evidence of what students are learning by reading the charts they have created. Charts stay up during the instructional time for units you are teaching. Charts come down when units are finished, but don't throw the charts away! I discovered from several of my Dream Teachers that students like to take the charts home! That is proof for me that students really feel ownership of their learning when they love the charts that much!

Charts are a valuable learning tool for students to refer to when they are working independently.

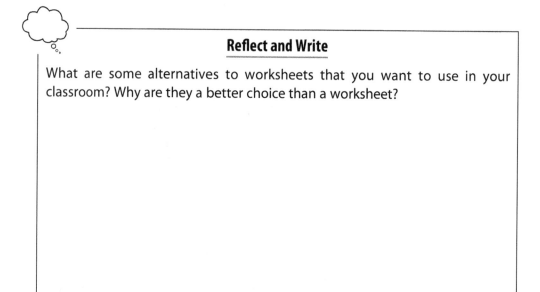

Reflect and Write

What are some alternatives to worksheets that you want to use in your classroom? Why are they a better choice than a worksheet?

Literacy Strategies Across the Curriculum

Teaching Literacy doesn't stop after English Language Arts lessons are over. A Dream Teacher teaches literacy throughout the day during every subject and every activity. Students read for information in Social Studies and Science. They apply their critical thinking, problem solving, and numeracy skills in Mathematics. Writing to inform, to persuade, and express their views and feelings are key to every subject. Literacy skills will carry students through life and open the door to their future. Whether your students speak English or other languages the formula is simple. The more students read, and the more students write, the better their reading and writing will be. Giving them opportunities to apply their literacy skills across all the content areas will extend their ELA class throughout the day.

Reading Content Textbooks

Most districts have a textbook for Social Studies and/or Science. Reading the content in a textbook can be somewhat daunting for students. However, reading texts with dense content is an important reading skill. Reading for information is a reading skill that must be taught and practiced. Using reading strategies, combined with note taking, is a valuable skill for your students to learn.

Never Read the Textbook to Students!

There are a variety of reading strategies to help your students to unlock key information from their textbooks and informational articles. When students are confronted with text many teachers' first impulse is to read the text to them. This is never a good idea! When you read to students they are not attempting to read the text themselves. Students who are not auditory learners will not receive the information when it is being read to them. Students need to learn strategies to read the text together with a group, with a buddy, and eventually independently.

No Round Robin Reading!

When a teacher calls on one student at a time to read there are 24 other students that are sitting and listening, or not. Round Robin reading is never acceptable in large groups, or small groups. Children need to practice reading with support so they can improve their reading. So whether you pick a name on a stick out of a cup, or do pop-corn reading, it is still a version of Round Robin reading. Teach children the strategies they need for reading text and give them lots of opportunities and time to do it!

Reading Strategies

Pre-Read the Text

Together with the students look at the text features in the section or chapter they will read. Helping students read the table of contents, captions under photos and pictures, headings and sub headings will help them to preview the information. Reading tables and charts are also key to understanding the content and information being presented.

Review the Vocabulary

Most texts have vocabulary highlighted throughout the text. Create a word bank with the class using these important vocabulary words. A word bank is a specialized word wall for the content areas. You can create a simple one with the class through a vocabulary charting activity. This chart will be displayed throughout the unit and words can be added.

Reading the Text

Now that students understand how to use the text features and have reviewed the vocabulary they are ready to start reading. Depending on your grade level some of your students may be able to read the text independently. That is the goal for all students! If students need support with the text try one of the following reading strategies.

- **Choral Reading**—Short sections of the text can be read together. The teacher leads the read to model fluency, students read along orally. This can be done whole group or small group.
- **Buddy Reading**—Students read together with a reading buddy. Each student takes a turn reading a paragraph or a page of text, while the other student listens and provides support as needed.
- **Small Group Reading**—A teacher or assistant can read the text together with a small group of students that need additional support. Reading together chunks of text chorally and discussing what has been read can be a powerful learning strategy for struggling students.

Taking Notes

Students benefit from reading text and taking notes of key points. There are a variety of note taking strategies you may want to teach your students. I recommend that they keep their notes in their content journal or mini book. Cornell notes are an efficient way for students to take notes and write a short summary of their learning.

Cornell Notes	
Topic and Date: (Before Reading)	
Cues: (After Reading) Central Ideas, Vocabulary, Key Points	**Notes:** (During Reading) Key Words and Ideas, Important Dates, People, and Places, Diagrams
Summary: (After Reading)	

Instructional Read Alouds

Students in every grade level benefit by being read to. Even students in the upper grades enjoy picture books with compelling and meaningful stories connected to what they are learning. Hearing good literature, poetry, and informational articles read fluently is an excellent way for students to learn about topics being studied. When the teacher reads to their students from selections connected to their content area they build students' background information. Teachers can read text that is above their student's grade level that will add interest and enjoyment to their lessons.

Children of all ages enjoy being read to from beautiful picture books. Today there are picture books to tell stories about difficult times in history, famous people who have made a mark on history and the arts, and folk tales and stories about people from around the world. Explore your library when you begin a new topic of study and choose compelling books and stories to share with students about the topic. Add these books to your reading corner for students to enjoy and read independently.

> **How to create an Instructional Read-Aloud:**
>
> 1. Choose a book that has a great story or message.
> 2. Identify the standard and focus for your lesson that fits with the story.
> 3. Read the story and write a summary.
> 4. Plan your introduction. How will you "hook" the kids to get them excited about the story?
> 5. Write six questions to use throughout the story and after reading.
> 6. Plan a follow-up activity to give students an opportunity to demonstrate their learning.
> 7. Practice reading the story before you read it to your students!

Using Resources and Technology

Resources are the tools students need to support their learning, technology is a tool. Weston Kieschnick, author of *Bold School*, says, "A computer will never be able to replace the caring relationship and mutual respect of authority you can establish with each of your students." He is so right! Back in the day I remember hearing about computers coming into the classroom and some teachers were worried that we would be out of a job. We had a vision of the Jetsons and thought students in the future would all be taught by robots. Well of course, that never happened. Weston is right. Nothing can replace the heart of a teacher. So when you choose technology tools remember that they are just a tool. You are the teacher! Technology is an awesome tool, kids generally love technology, and they will use technology tools throughout their lives, but it is still just a tool for learning and communication.

The resources you will use will range from a wide variety of books, games, models, manipulatives, and technology. Whatever you choose must be readily accessible for students to use and directly applicable to the work the students will be doing. Giving students a choice of the resources they use can add interest and individuality to the work your students produce. Some students may want to share information in an informative book, or report. Other students may want to create a PowerPoint presentation, a skit or an interview. Depending on what the outcome you have in mind may be for the lesson it is important to provide students with the resources they will need to support their learning. Keep a balance in your classroom by using a variety of resources and giving students an opportunity to use and explore a variety of new tools!

Differentiation

Students are all different and sometimes it may seem impossible to differentiate instruction to meet their learning needs. Here are some tips to help you differentiate instruction for your students. Keep in mind that the whole group lesson is for everyone. Differentiation most often happens when it is time to apply the standard. Most students will do the assignment connected to the lesson that you have planned. You can give an alternative assignment that is connected to the standard that is either above, or below grade level. Think of differentiation when you plan whole group, small group, and one on one instruction. Students are all doing assignments connected to the standard, but at varying levels of application. Use formative assessment to determine who needs additional help and who will benefit from a more challenging assignment. Once students have met the success criteria it will be time to move on to the next lesson!

Planning the Lesson

Once you have determined the standard you are going to teach, and you have chosen the teaching strategies you will use in your lesson, the next step is planning the lesson. Planning a good lesson is your script for delivering great instruction. Your planning is intentional and focused on student learning. Planning the lesson will give you the confidence you need to actually present the lesson to your students.

A good lesson has a *beginning*, a *middle*, and an *end*. It seems so simple, but it is true! Your lesson should begin by telling students what they are going to learn and getting them excited about the lesson. The middle of the lesson is the time when you begin to gradually release students to work independently to apply their learning, and the end wraps the lesson up and gives students an opportunity to demonstrate what they have learned.

Assess the Outcome

Formative Assessments—Before/During/After
A formative assessment is an assessment that is created and used by the classroom teacher to form an opinion about student learning. Teachers do a variety of formative assessments all day long. A formative assessment strategy can even be thought of as "Kid Watching." As soon as your students

come into the classroom you are assessing their readiness for learning. While students are working on assignments, or on the carpet for discussion, a good teacher is watching students to determine if they are understanding. Good "Kid Watching" will guide the lesson, and show you where you may want to change or adapt the lesson you have planned.

A teacher is constantly assessing his or her students throughout the lesson. Watching your students, talking to them about their learning throughout the lesson and providing feedback has high impact on student engagement and student learning. Assessment happens throughout every lesson so you can provide support, assistance, and even adjustments that will help you to meet the individual needs of every student.

When I am teaching I like to use individual white boards so students can record their answers and hold them up so I can instantly see who is meeting the learning objective. Thumbs up, thumbs down is also an easy way to see instantly my students' understanding of what I am teaching. When I am conferring with students I keep anecdotal notes so I can remember and look back at my assessment and goal for that student.

At the end of the lesson you will want to do a final review to determine whether or not your students met the success criteria. There are a variety of ways you can assess students at the end of the lesson that are quick and will give you the information you need for planning next steps for instruction. One common way to find out what students know is to provide an "Exit Ticket" to each student to respond to and turn in at the end of the lesson. Reviewing the exit tickets will help you to determine next steps and inform your teaching for the following day. You can also use the student activity as a form of assessment. Does their completed product show that they have met the success criteria for the standard and objective that was taught? Assessing learning is the most important step to good teaching and is essential to delivering good instruction. Use the information to inform your lessons going forward.

Reflect and Write

List formative assessment strategies that you could use in your classroom.

Reflect and Write

How will assessments and assessment data help me to know my students and plan lessons that will meet each of their individual needs?

Reflect and Write

How will I use whole group, small group, and one on one instruction to meet students' needs?

Plan your Dream Classroom Lesson, Step by Step!

Now it is time to plan your Dream Classroom lesson! Work individually or with a partner to go through the steps for planning that follow. The steps for planning are listed below. Use the Lesson Planning Map to guide you as you plan your lesson.

   Step 1—Identify the standard being taught
   Step 2—Create a learning objective and a student friendly "I Can" statement.
   Step 3—Determine the teaching strategy you will use to teach the lesson.
   Step 4—Choose a student activity that will match the standard and show their learning.

Step 5—Plan for differentiation. (How will I adapt the lesson for students who need support?)
Step 6—Identify resources needed.
Step 7—Assessment—How will I know that students have met the learning objective?
Step 8—After the lesson is completed, reflect—What went well? What is the next step? What will I do different next time?

Choose one standard that you are going to teach and complete the Lesson Planning Map below:

Lesson Planning Map	
1. Subject, grade level, and Standard(s)	
2. Learning Objective I-Can Statement	
3. Teaching Strategies	
4. Student Activities	
5. Differentiation	
6. Resources Needed	
7. Assessment	

Think about your lesson and what it will look like, sound like, and feel like. How will you present the standard and objective of the lesson and get students excited to learn? How will you provide instruction and modeling to teach the objective? How will you gradually release the lesson through targeted student activities for students to learn and practice the standard being taught? And finally, how will you assess the lesson to know what your students have learned? You have identified what and how you want to teach the standard on your planning Map. Now let's take that plan and turn it into a real lesson plan.

Creating a Three-Part Lesson to provide Gradual Release to Students: I Do, We Do, You Do

The Beginning of the Lesson—I Do

How you begin your lesson will determine the level of engagement and understanding your students will have. Think about your presentation. How will you make this lesson relevant to students? What will be your "Hook" to get students excited about the lesson? The beginning of the lesson will include introducing the standard and *I can* statement. Students need to know what they are going to learn, what they are going to do, and how they will know when they have been successful. This is where you get them hooked into learning. A quick review of the previous lesson or lessons will help them to make a connection to build on their learning. Posing a rhetorical question, sharing a quick scenario, or even a song or a video clip are also ways that you can get students focused on new learning. The beginning of the lesson is the part of the lesson where the teacher sets the stage and ignites the learning. This part of the lesson is often referred to as "I Do."

Reflect and Write

Write your ideas below for the beginning of your lesson.

Middle of the Lesson—We Do

The students are ready to learn and now you will guide them through the lesson. This is where you will choose high impact teaching strategies to empower students to learn and master the success criteria for the standard. If you are teaching a Math lesson you may want to use direct instruction to teach the concept and provide a worked example as a model for students so they know what success looks like. The middle of your lesson will move quickly from "I Do" to "We Do" as your lesson becomes interactive. Interactive charting is a good strategy to get students engaged in learning. Once again, a chart is a worked example for students to use as a guide when they begin to work in small groups, pairs, and independently. The middle of the lesson is the time students are learning together with their peers and with you. Some students will move quickly to the independent stage, or *You Do*. Some students will need more time and support and will stay in this stage a bit longer. If your students need more time to practice before they can do a task independently add "Two Do" to the process. When students work together with a partner they will gain confidence as they move to the "You Do" or independent stage.

Reflect and Write

Write your ideas below for the middle of your lesson.

End of the Lesson—You Do

During the middle and toward the end of the lesson is the time when students will begin to transition to the independent, or *You Do*, stage of gradual release. Students may arrive at the independent stage at different times. Some students may still need additional support and time to work with a partner before they are ready to work independently. Once you see that most students are able to work independently you can move into the *You Do* stage. While most students are working independently you can provide one on one or small group instruction to those who need additional support.

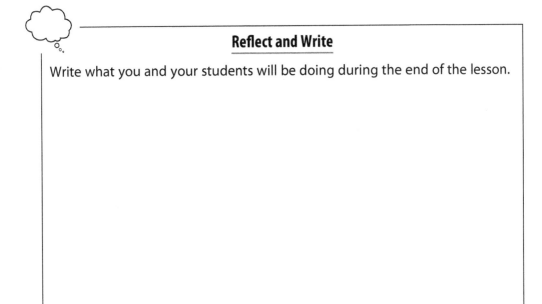

Reflect and Write

Write what you and your students will be doing during the end of the lesson.

Closing the Lesson

When work time is over it is important to pull the whole group back to actually close the lesson. The lesson may continue the following day, but students need to reflect on their learning and know what the next steps will be tomorrow. The close of the lesson is just as important as the beginning of the lesson. Refer back to the learning objective and the *I Can* statement to remind students of what they learned. Using student work, an exit ticket, or any other form of assessment will help you and your students to know if they have been successful.

Now it is time for you to plan your own Dream Lesson! You can use the template provided, or your own. Whatever template you choose make sure to use the Lesson Planning Map and ideas from this chapter to create and plan your Dream Lesson!

Three-Part Lesson Planning Template
Standard/I Can Statement/Success Criteria (Student Activity)
Resources Needed
Beginning
Middle
End
Assessment

Don't Ever Give up Your Dream!

You have worked hard to go through the steps of becoming a Dream Teacher, in your very own Dream Classroom! Planning great lessons, discovering great new learning strategies, and trying new student activities is an ongoing part of being a Dream Teacher. This chapter and book have provided you with many ideas and hopefully you will have success as you give them a try. Remember that you are learning, and just like students, you will have times when you feel successful, and times that you will think that you have failed. Teaching is both an art and a science, it takes your own ideas and special flair to make lessons come alive!

Don't be discouraged if a lesson doesn't go as well as you expected or hoped. I have learned the most from some of my lessons that failed! Teaching is a work in progress and you will get better and better as you continue trying new strategies. If you try a new teaching strategy and it doesn't work think about what happened and how you can improve it for the next time. It takes practice to put new teaching strategies into place. Give yourself permission to fail and time to improve and master the new strategy over time. Becoming a Dream Teacher is a process, and creating Dream Lessons will be part of your life long journey!

Tips from the Pros!

What ideas or advice to you have for developing teachers that will help them to deliver effective instruction?

Claudia Use thematic teaching whenever you can to incorporate music, art, and movement, across the curriculum. This makes learning more fun and covers those students with different interests. Balance phonics with reading GOOD literature to keep students motivated and expose them to a variety of genres. I recommend Fountas & Pinnell for teaching reading!

Marion Feedback—effective feedback for each individual student!

Dawn Marie I use Kagen Structures to check to see that my kids are building strong connections with their teams and with their classrooms. I start with Pair/Share activities.

Gail Reflection . . . John Dewey said, "We do not learn from experience . . . we learn from reflecting on experience." Every activity time needs to include reflection time.

Chelsea I love doing Read Alouds with my students and I find books that will connect to the lessons and get my kids excited about learning. They enjoy stories and we do a story map together after each one.

Mick

- If kids get a sense you don't like them forget it, they won't learn from you!

- Boys easily get lost if they don't have structure or boundaries. They need to know what is expected and why they are learning it! Also, don't forget that boys learn best through hands-on and active learning activities.

- Break up your lessons into manageable pieces so the kids can understand. Small bits are easier to swallow!

- Let kids know that it doesn't matter if you messed up today, tomorrow is a new day!

Lynne You have to have a sense of humor! Don't take things personally!

John

- My students loved it when I would give them scenarios to prepare skits and act them out. They loved expressing themselves and I learned as much as they did from the performances!

- I loved reading to my students and we especially enjoyed books by authors who had a sense of humor! Roald Dahl was one of our favorites!

- Catch your students being good and let them know!

- Let your students know you like them and build relationships.

Jean Critical thinking is "Critical" for the adult world our students are entering and especially for the sophisticated jobs technology is creating! I recommend the book *Making Thinking Visible*, by Ron Richard, Mark Church, and Karin Morrison. These strategies are highly engaging for students and can begin in grade 1!

Carole Math problem solving strategies provide the tools students can use and give them the opportunity to use a variety of ways to solve problems. Also use Socratic Questioning, a great way to dig deeper and guides students in developing critical thinking.

> **Claudia** Use Centers and Cooperative Learning in teams. The "We all swim or sink" concept sure helps students learn to think of others and not just themselves! Also, teach thematically and use as many of the Multiple Intelligences Activities as possible to stimulate all kinds of learners.

Discussion Questions

1. What high impact teaching strategies did you learn that were new to you? What ones are you going to try?
2. How is gradual release connected to a Three-Part Lesson?
3. What are some ideas that you want to try as an alternative to a worksheet?
4. Why is it important to start and end every lesson with the objective, or "I Can" statement and the success criteria? Why would it be beneficial to refer to the objective throughout the lesson?
5. Why is assessment important throughout the lesson and at the end? What are some simple ways to assess students' understanding?
6. What ideas did you like from the "Tips from the Pros?"

> ## Notes to Trainers and Mentors
> Your district may have special requirements for lesson planning and templates for teachers to use. Spend time reviewing the requirements with teachers and provide assistance as needed. Lesson planning is often the most challenging and time-consuming task that your teachers will face so any guidance you can give them will be greatly appreciated! Encourage grade level teams to work together to ease the load and work toward consistency across the grade level.

Self Assessment

Check the boxes that match you!

I am familiar with my grade level standards and use them to write my lessons.	
I share the objective, or student friendly, "I Can" statement at the beginning, throughout, and at the end of the lesson.	
I choose high impact strategies that will increase student learning.	
I am clear about what is expected and provide a model for students.	
My lessons have a beginning, middle, and end. I use formative assessment strategies to check my students' understanding and adjust my lesson as needed.	
My lessons are relevant to students and fun!	

My Next Steps

Keep Your Dream Classroom Alive

You have worked hard to create your Dream Classroom. Your classroom environment is inviting and motivating students to learn. Your routines and procedures are in place and students are following them routinely. You have planned good lessons and the day is packed with teaching and learning. Your class is your little family and you are enjoying your students. In addition, you are attending meetings before and after school, supervising students at recess, and communicating with parents, planning instruction, the list goes on. But how can you keep it going? When do you have time for yourself and your own family? This is a question that teachers have faced throughout history. Teacher burnout is real, and we don't want it to happen to you! There are ways for you to balance your school life, and your home life. In this chapter we will look at ways to support you, the Dream Teacher!

Manage Your Health

You have dreamed of being a teacher since you were a child. This is your perfect job and it is what you have always wanted to do. But nobody ever told you it was going to be this hard, did they? We teachers tend to be over achievers and we see ourselves as super heroes that can solve everyone's problems. But the truth is, we are only people, and we can't do it all.

Stress is real and we need to take care of ourselves. The Robert Wood Johnson Foundation from Penn State has researched the topic of stress in teaching and the results are alarming. Did you know that 30–40 percent of new teachers leave the profession by the 5th year? Of the teachers surveyed, 46 percent reported high daily stress, which compromises their health, sleep, quality of life, and teaching performance (*Teacher Stress and Health*, Robert Wood Johnson Foundation, Sept 1, 2016). So the question is, what can you do to make sure you don't become a statistic? How will you keep all the plates spinning and have a smile on your face? It isn't easy, but it can be done! Believe it or not, it begins with taking care of yourself!

Eat Right

You know as well as I do your health should be a priority. But how many of us get into bad habits that erode our good health little by little. When I was a first-year teacher I was so overwhelmed that I got into a cycle of bad eating habits that have actually haunted me for a lifetime. As a single woman, with my first job, I felt the pressure and worked long hours. I didn't even think about grocery shopping. Who has time to make a healthy lunch? I sure didn't. So, as a result I ate school lunch, healthy right? I started my day with the drive-through to my favorite coffee shop for my coffee and a couple of donuts. On my way home I grabbed some fast food to eat while I laid on the couch and watched TV. I look back at it now and realize that I was stressed, tired, and worn out. Of course I gained some weight, I had no energy, and my back to school wardrobe was getting a little tight.

I woke up one day and realized my pattern had to change. It started first with the school lunch routine. I began packing my own lunch with a healthy sandwich or salad, fruit, and my own water or diet soda. It was actually more relaxing to eat my lunch with teachers or in my classroom rather than the cafeteria. Even as a consultant today I do my best to take my own bottle of water and healthy snacks to eat during the day. Taking time to relax and eat, socialize with colleagues, or just enjoy some peace and quiet, is a gift you can give to yourself. Taking control of what you eat is a great first step to being a healthy and active teacher!

You may be thinking that this is a great idea but you can't imagine how you can do it with your busy schedule. Keep in mind that anytime you are doing something positive for yourself, you are also doing something positive for your students and your family. Plan your meals and your lunches. Make a list of healthy foods you want to eat and schedule a routine trip to the grocery store. Think of what you what you want to stock in your refrigerator at home and at school. Many teachers I work with have a refrigerator in their classroom to keep their lunches and healthy snacks. Some teachers even have a hot pot and a little microwave of their own to prepare their own coffee and warm up food. This may be a good investment for you, especially if you struggle with your weight and healthy eating. Stocking up your little refrigerator with your healthy drinks and snacks on Monday will carry you through the week. Creating your own little healthy corner in the room is an investment in yourself. You are important and this is one way to take care of yourself! You are also modeling good habits for your students. We all struggle with healthy eating in our world today, so why don't you be the role model for your students as you show them how you are making good healthy choices!

Reflect and Write

What are your routines for eating and drinking healthy food during the day? Is there at least one area that you would like to improve? Write down two healthy changes you would like to make to your eating habits!

Take a Walk

We all know that exercise is vital to our overall health, but most of us don't do it! One of the best ways to handle stress it to exercise. For me it was walking. Early in my career I started to take walks before or after school. It feels good to get outside in the fresh air. Being close to nature is a natural stress reliever. I have continued walking throughout my career. Getting in at least 10,000 steps a day is easy when I count the steps I make all day at school. Your students will also love to walk! I often asked my students to join me and we took walks together during recess. We kept track of our laps around the track and challenged ourselves to see how many laps we could complete each day. When I became a principal, I started walking clubs for students to enjoy!

You might even want to exercise together with staff at your school. My colleagues and I often took exercise classes together. We enjoyed aerobic dancing and at one point we even had a dance instructor deliver a class for us at school! Now I enjoy going to the gym and doing water aerobics. Whatever kind of exercise you enjoy, find a way to work that into your own schedule and routine. Consider including your own passion with your students! Build exercise opportunities into your school day. A walk with your students, spontaneous dance party, and even yoga, will help you and your students to become healthier and eliminate stress!

Reflect and Write

What exercise do you enjoy? How can you include exercise and physical movement into your weekly schedule and school day?

School is School—Home is Home

Teachers feel constantly torn between their home and family, and their classroom and students. There is always something to be attended to at both places. If you are a parent this is a huge problem. The first thing to recognize is your family comes first. We often forget this and it can be devastating if we don't find a way to create a balance in our life. Teachers often take work home with them, and even worse, the emotional baggage we carry takes our focus off our own family. The question is, how can a *Dream Teacher* support his or her students at school and still have the time and emotional energy left for their families at home?

Manage Your Time

Time management is important in any profession, but for a teacher it can become even a greater issue. There is always something to be done! We try to do it all, but it is an impossible task. Effective teachers embrace organization. I have yet to meet a highly effective teacher who doesn't have an organizational system. The key is to find what works for YOU, and not try to adopt a system that doesn't fit your style. So how do you manage your time?

When I was a single teacher I had all the time in the world to spend at school. I worked after school, before school, and even went to school on Saturday if I had extra work to do. However, as I became more aware of what was expected of me, and I had a family, I found ways to plan and use my time that was more streamlined and efficient. Here are some ideas that worked for me:

1. **Report cards**—The key to report cards was to keep up with grading. Daily work was always graded together with students. Not only was this more time efficient, students became aware of their own success and areas of need. I found ways to make this positive and comfortable for students. Letting them check their own paper was important. Writing their grade on their paper and turning it in for me to record the grade was one way to save time, and also save face. I reviewed their paper and recorded their grades before I returned them to students. This was also a great way for me to assess student progress and plan for targeted instruction to meet their individual needs. Collecting grades does not have to be daily, but you do need to have enough grades to report a fair assessment of a students work for each subject.
2. **Pacing your time**—When I had report cards to do I tried to divide up my time and do a little each day. Sometimes I came up with a system and marked one section of each card at a time. For instance, I might figure all the Math grades and record the marks all at one time. Other times I figured all of the grades and did two to three cards a day until the cards were finished. Of course it's not a good idea to procrastinate and do them at the last minute.
3. **Lesson planning**—I planned a little bit for the following week each day, but I always stayed after school on Thursday to complete my plans and gather resources for the next week. Thursday was my "late" day. That worked well for me and I felt good leaving the building on the clock time every other day, because I knew I would stay late on Thursday. Those afternoon work sessions were productive for me and I maintained that schedule for most of my teaching career. Even later when I became a school administrator I kept Thursday after school as *My Time* to get my work done!
4. **Planning time**—I felt on top of things when I used my planning time to *plan*! This takes a lot of discipline and I encourage you to

use your free time to get your work done at school. Planning time can be quickly eaten up by meetings and catching up on correspondence. As much as possible keep that time sacred and do your work! It is easy to get distracted during your planning time, and before you know it the students are back in your classroom. Become disciplined and use your planning time wisely.

5. **Don't take it home**—*Home is home* and *school is school*. When you get the two confused it never turns out well. There were times I took work home and it sat on the counter all weekend. Use your time wisely at school so that you don't have to take work home. You wouldn't think of taking your laundry to school, would you? Separate your home life from your school life and you will be happier!

6. **Or take it home**—On the other hand some of you might just focus better at home once you've had a chance to step away from the school setting. The key is to attempt to balance it all. If taking it home works better for you then go ahead and take it home. It may give you a feeling of confidence working on it in peace surrounded by your own four walls!

7. **Streamline the classroom environment**—The boards in my classroom were general and the base of them didn't change all year. What changed was the student work, charts, posters, and other visual representations of the current topics we were studying in class. I hated putting up paper backing on the board and got permission to paint my boards a pretty light blue. The light blue background worked for every subject and was fresh all year! My centers were well organized and easy for students to help manage. My classroom library was also nicely organized so students could take care of their books and put them back in the right spot! Think about ways you can streamline your classroom when you set it up at the beginning of the year. This will save you hours of work later on!

8. **Give students responsibility**—My students had jobs, and they were important jobs that I expected them to do! Some of the jobs were done in the morning, throughout the day, and everyone had jobs to do at the end of the day. The key to making this work is to make it "visible." Creating a Job Board with students and rotating the assignments builds a sense of classroom community and pride. In one school I supported, the principal

awarded the Golden Dustpan to one classroom each month following her walk-through inspection. She wore maintenance coveralls and carried a broom and clipboard into classrooms on unannounced visits to determine monthly winners. Very clever! When my students left the classroom to go home my classroom was in order. I had a teacher assistant, a librarian, center managers, and a variety of other jobs that my students loved to do. Students enjoyed having responsibility for their classroom and it gave me extra time to do the work that I needed to do!

So now it is your turn. Think of what you have to do throughout a normal school day. You plan and prepare lessons, you gather resources, you post the daily schedule and standards, and add to, or change, boards, centers, and stations in your classroom environment. In addition, you have communication to parents in the form of emails, texts, phone calls, and class newsletters that takes a chunk of your precious time every day. And of course, you also have staff meetings, planning meetings, student meetings, and training that is mandatory. Just thinking about all of it can make your head spin. So how do you, the Dream Teacher, get it all done? A good start is to look at what you have to do, and find ways you can do it in the most efficient way!

Make a list of what you do throughout the school day below:

Jobs I am doing now	**Ways I can streamline the work I have to do!**
Sorting assignments by subject that have been turned in	**Assign my student assistant to sort assignments and put them in a folder for each subject.**

Now look at your list and see if there are ways you can streamline, or even eliminate, certain tasks. Can students or volunteers help? Can you share planning with your team? Can you eliminate any of the jobs? Think about ways you can streamline your work and make your life easier!

Manage Your Stress

Life is stressful and when you are working full time it can be double stressful. Teacher's face more stress than most other occupations so you must learn how to manage stress. It isn't just the amount of work that has to be done that can cause you to feel stressed out, it is also the pressure we face and the emotional toll of being a teacher in charge of 25 students that makes us feel stressed out. We are people persons, and we interact with people all day long. On most days and with most people it is a positive experience, but sometimes we can get begin to feel anxious when there is too much coming at us at once. Here are some ideas to help you with the stress of interacting with people all day long.

1. Be polite and acknowledge everyone you see, but keep it short if you feel a need to be in your classroom getting work done.
2. Stay away from areas where there is a lot of people and chatter if you have work to do. That usually means the teachers' lounge and the office!
3. Playing music in your classroom before students arrive or after students leave for the day can be a real stress reliever. Turn on your iTunes and enjoy music that soothes your soul. Music that motivates or renews you is pretty powerful!
4. Surround yourself with positive people. Don't let negative Nellies get you down!
5. Be positive—Being positive and having a positive attitude is a choice that you make. It is so easy to respond to situations and speak in a negative way. Try to catch yourself when you hear yourself being negative
6. Keep out of it—There are sometimes issues that are happening at the school. When this happens everyone loves to talk, and most of it is gossip. The best rule of thumb is to put on your blinders and keep out of it. If it doesn't involve you directly turn your head the other way. Some people love drama, don't be one of those people.

7. The best way to eliminate stress is to focus on your students! When you spend time with your students it will take your mind off whatever is stressing you out and even bring you joy!
8. When you are stressed, your students may be feeling stressed, too! Turn on fun video apps like GoNoodle! Dancing, singing, and having a good laugh, is not only fun, but a great way to relieve stress!

Reflect and Write

What stresses you out? What are some ideas to help me to eliminate and handle the stress I feel being a teacher?

The Technology Blues

I will admit it, I am trapped by my technology and social networking. This is the modern way of life and we have all grabbed it with gusto. Technology has a positive impact on our lives. We can stay in touch with people all over the world. We can Google whatever we want to know. We can shop, and merchandise magically shows up at our homes. We can communicate with our friends and loved ones in an instant. And of course, we use technology for our professional lives as well. We now have our books on line, we can keep our lesson plans and grades on line, all of our data is at our finger tips in an instant. However wonderful technology is, it can still cause us a great deal of stress. I call this stress the Technology Blues! So how do we manage the stress of technology? Here are some ideas that may help you!

1. You may not be able to turn your phone off during the school day, but you sure can put the ringer on silent. Whenever you hear a ping or a ring, your blood pressure will rise. No matter how hard you try to ignore it you are still wondering who it is and what do they want. Turn off the ringer and put the phone

in your desk or cupboard and lock it up while you are teaching if you can!
2. Check your Facebook and do your on-line shopping at home. Social networking at school will eat up the time you have to plan and get the work done in your classroom that you need to do. It is amazing how much time we can waste on our phones!
3. When technology doesn't work it is extremely frustrating, especially when we have important work to do. If you can't figure something out you will need a "go to" person to help you. Knowing the techie gurus in your building is essential! If you are the techie guru in your building, then Bless you!
4. Don't create lessons that totally depend on technology. You may have the greatest video clip to show the kids, or fun game or activity to play with them on the smart board, but if the internet is down you are stuck! Make sure to have a back-up plan for technology lessons! Fussing with the computer and smart board to get it going can detract from your lesson and you will lose your students' interest. If it doesn't work teach the lesson the old fashioned, but dependable, way! Use the white board, chart paper, or engage students with an alternative activity. Your stress and theirs will go down!

Reflect and Write

How much time do I spend using technology for personal reasons during the school day? What are my biggest frustrations with technology? What can I do to eliminate stress that is caused by the Technology Blues?

Build Your Circle of Friends

Creating school friendships is one of the most important ways for you to manage stress. You will spend a lot of time at your school and the friends you make there will provide support for you in many ways. However, to make friends you have to reach out and first be a friend. Knock on the door of the classrooms near yours and meet your colleagues. Offer to help them when they are rearranging furniture or unpacking boxes. Work together with your team and step up to the plate when there is something extra that needs to be done. Your kindness and willingness to help will come back to you twofold. My best friends in life have been the ones I worked with. Many of us became friends at school and later were friends outside of school. During difficult times in my personal life it was my school friends that reached out to me. Your friends become your own little school family. Find ways to make connections and reach out to people. I guarantee you that it is the friends you make at school that will provide you the safety net you will need throughout your teaching career and your life!

Here I am with my dearest friend, Vickie. We started teaching together when we were young and single. We celebrated each other's weddings, the birth of our children, and supported each other through thick and thin. There's nothing like a good friend to help you grow and support you throughout your teaching career!

Reflect and Write

How do you and your colleagues support each other at school? What more could you and your team do to provide a network of support among the staff?

Have Some Fun!

A Dream Teacher knows how to have fun! It is important to have fun in your life to help keep your life in balance. When we take life too seriously it never turns out good. There are times that you will be stressed and your students will be stressed, too! After testing, several days of indoor recess and working hard to finish a big project are just some examples of things that will stress you and your students out. So, what can you plan with your class that is fun? Game Days, Pyjama and Read Days, Dance Parties, and a special treat are ways you can have fun with your students. A Dream Teacher can sense when students need a break. Bringing fun into your classroom is a great way to reduce stress for yourself and your students!

But how about you? When is the last time you really had fun? Adult fun is important, and it helps us all to deal with stress. We all have a different definition of fun. Maybe you need a night out with your friends, a round of golf, or a movie to have fun. Outings with your friends and family will take your mind off work. Having fun with your colleagues at school is also important. I remember the fun I had at one school when we put on a Teacher Talent Show for the students. This became an annual event and the kids loved it. There is nothing more fun than singing and dancing with your friends at school. I know it sounds crazy, but sometimes crazy fun is just what we need!

Seek Peace

We all need quiet time to recharge our brains, our minds, and our hearts. Rest is important to our overall good health, but it is vital to help us to maintain our sanity during stressful times. Getting enough sleep is crucial to our performance at school, at home, and in our lives. In addition to restful sleep we also need quiet time to meditate or pray to connect with our spiritual self. Some people I know have improved their health and wellness of mind and body through yoga. If that is for you make time into your schedule to go to classes at home or at a yoga studio. If you are a spiritual person make sure you practice your faith and include worship and prayer into your daily and weekly routine. You may want to find a way to seek peace that works for you. When you are stressed your quiet time and meditation will help you to recharge and handle the stress of your busy life.

Ask For Help

Whether you are a new teacher, or a teacher with many years under your belt, there will be times when you need support. The stress of teaching combined with the stress of our personal lives can take a toll on even the best *Dream Teacher*. Don't ever be afraid to ask for help when you need it. Your colleagues will be there for you and your principal, too, if you let them know that you are having a tough time. There is no shame to needing help because we have all been there. When you need support all you have to do is ask. Sharing your heart with someone that is close to you is an important step to getting the support you desperately need. Don't feel ashamed or embarrassed to ask, we have all been there.

Goal Setting and a Promise to Yourself!

Set a goal to help you to be healthy and to handle stress. Create a plan to make that happen, and then make a promise to yourself that you will stick with the plan! If you decide you don't ever want to take work home—then make a plan so that can happen. The next step is to make a promise to yourself that you will follow the plan. When you make a plan and a promise to stay focused and take care of yourself you can be a Dream Teacher at home and at school! Review your reflections from this chapter. Determine the most important areas that you would like to focus so that you can keep your Dream Classroom, without causing stress to yourself! List each goal and, make a plan to keep that goal, and then make a promise to yourself!

My Goal	My Plan	My Promise

Congratulations! You are becoming the Dream Teacher you always wanted to be!

I hope this book has given you the steps to guide you as you create your Dream Classroom. Please remember that it is a journey and there will always be challenges as you learn how to create a classroom where children can feel safe, confident, and loved. This is the basic need for all children to be successful in school and you are the person who can make that happen. You are a Dream Teacher because you made the choice to step into the lives of the children you teach. Take care of yourself, take care of your students, and don't forget what it feels like to be a child. Don't worry if you are not perfect, none of us are. Your heart for your students and your love of teaching is what is important. Remember, when you walk into your classroom, YOU are the Dream Teacher that can make a difference to the lives of the children you teach every day!

Tips from the Pros!

Karen

- Find one specific colleague who is a "Safe Zone." In other words, sometimes you just need to talk something out, and it might not be positive, but it helps to complain sometimes. I would go to Michelle and say, "I need a Safe Zone moment." She knew that meant I needed to get something off my chest, and her primary role was to listen, and not spread any of what I said outside of our partner bond. I did the same for her. We had each other's backs, and knew we were in safe zone regarding confidence.

- Find humor in your own mistakes. Students love to point out mistakes you make, we have fun with it and turn it into a joke when it happens!

- Remain diverse. Even if you think you'll never want to teach anything but 2nd grade, step out of your comfort zone and welcome new experiences with ELL, Special Education, and alternate grade level opportunities. Shift roles, classrooms, and buildings, and embrace changes that keep you "fresh" and "best" for students who need you.

- When my own children were young and I was a full-time teacher, I would pick them up from day-care or school, and when we first got home, I would set a timer for 40 minutes of play with them. No TV, no homework, no laundry, no school planning or grading. It was our time together. At the timer, I started dinner while they started homework, or could play with each other, or could help me with dinner. Both of my sons sat on the counter to mix or fix food, set the table, etc. They are both quite efficient adults now in the kitchen.

Jane

- I work really hard during the week, but I always take weekends completely off.

- I remember I have the power to change things that are not working for me or my students.

- I ask for help when I need it.

- I find the joy in my job.

- If I'm stressed I make a game or activity. The cutting, drawing, coloring, and gluing part of the job calms me.

Hannah

- I had a *Tomorrow* table with bins for each subject. At the end of each day, I went through tomorrow's lessons and pulled everything out in order of the day. That way when I left for the day I wasn't thinking about what needed to be done for tomorrow! This was also handy when by chance I went into labor or my child was sick! Everything was already there!

- I decided during my first year that I wouldn't bring anything home, after taking work home and never bringing it inside from the car! If it didn't get done that day, it could wait until tomorrow!
- Time away from school was MY time, and my family's. No checking email from Friday afternoon until Monday morning!

Krista When I was in the classroom, I would make sure I spent time with friends who didn't teach or work in schools. This way I wasn't tempted to talk about kids, work, job demands, etc. Now I take yoga classes to help to unplug from the day. I also book a massage once a month and get a facial every season. I book trips to look forward to. I do my best to make sure my job doesn't consume my entire life!

Marion Marking? Always a time-consuming task. Plan for marking when you plan the tasks, ensuring students know what you are marking for. Try peer marking, class marking, and whenever possible mark one on one with the student, giving feedback as you go along. Marking 30+ English essays at home is sometimes inevitable, but it needn't be the norm.

Claudia

- I stayed late to get ready for the next day and didn't take work home. Home was home and time for family and unplug. I also needed time outdoors to "cleanse" my mind. A run might take place at 5:00 a.m. or 10:00 p.m. but I did my best to make that happen every day!
- My best friend and teaching partner and I would go into school early some Saturday mornings to knock out big planning, while my family slept in. Or, I'd take my boys with a couple friends to play in the gym while I did planning on Sunday nights, both with a time limit. I never took work home!

Kim Just a small suggestion, and people who know me will laugh! When things seem to be getting out of control, find something that you can straighten up quickly. It might be a bookshelf, or a pile on the counter. Something you can see to remind yourself that you do have control!

Jean Set boundaries for yourself relative to the time you spend planning and following up so you can lead a balanced life. A life out of balance is not productive for you, your family, or your students. Have a regular schedule of exercise for yourself. A gym membership and classes like yoga, meditation, or dance can help structure a schedule for you.

Discussion Questions

1. What do you think causes the most stress for teachers in schools today? How does this contribute to teacher burnout?
2. What are some of the ideas to relieve stress that you want to try?
3. How could you and your team or school support each other to live a healthy life style?
4. What stood out to you as you read the ideas for relieving stress from the pros? Did you get any good ideas to try for yourself?
5. What is the biggest overall theme for living a balanced life that you heard reading this chapter?

Notes to Trainers and Mentors

Work together with your team to create ways to help your staff alleviate stress at work. In addition to fun activities, outings, and additional support you may want to consider putting a **Help Board** in the staff lounge. This board will be valuable as teachers' post, "I need a baby sitter on Saturday night?", "I need resources for a unit on frogs", etc. This board would be a great way to give staff real opportunities to support each other.

Another great idea to consider is a bulletin board that says, *"Catching Us at Our Best."* Staff can write positive comments and a thank-you to each other and post them on the board. This gives your staff a chance to "lift" their colleagues and support a common mission. Make sure it is for all the staff in the building. We are a team with our custodians, lunch personnel, parent volunteers, teachers, aides, and even our school administrators! Everyone will feel encouraged and appreciated when they see a note with *their* name on it!

Now that you have completed the chapters and activities in this book with your group it is time for a celebration! Have fun and remember, your teachers will need your continued support and guidance as they take what they have learned and put it into practice in their own Dream Classrooms!

Self Assessment

Check the boxes that match you!

I am working to balance my time between school and home.	
I am eating right and getting exercise to help me to stay physically and mentally fit.	
I use my work time at school to prepare and plan my lessons.	
I spend time with colleagues and friends that are supportive and positive.	
I have fun with my students.	
I enjoy activities that help me to relieve stress and do them on a regular basis.	
I reach out for support when I need it.	

My Next Steps

Thank-you Notes to Dream Teachers

Hopefully you have had at least one teacher that stands out in your mind that had a positive impact on your life. Most people have fond memories of their favorite teachers, so I asked my Facebook friends to post a thank-you to their favorite teachers. Here are some of the responses I received. As you read them think about how just the small things we do can have such a positive impact on a child's life! After you read these you may want to write a thank-you, to your favorite teacher!

Dear Mrs. Dunseth,

You loaned me a book of your own in the 6th grade and started a love affair with books for me. I wish I could remember the name of the book but I do remember it was about a girl the same age as me. In the early 1960s we didn't have all the wonderful selections for children like we do now and my family couldn't have afforded them anyway. I went on to major in English in college. I am now in my 60s and to this day I cannot be without a book wherever I go. I wish I could have told you thank you!

Ginger

Dear Ann Hirst,

When I burned through the, "I'm Done, what can I do next?" folder in short order, you encouraged me to visit the school library and design my own extended research projects delving deeper into topics that interested me. You allowed me to spend my recess with the 6th grade math class. You assured me that AV club should not be just a boy's activity. As I recall, you also good naturedly tolerated my satirical script writing collaboration with my bestie, Gretchen.

Ellie

Dear Mrs. Cool,

You came along at just the right time in my life. I had been a tomboy, all before Title Nine, so little sports outlet for girls. Your quiet smile to me made me feel confident in myself, having just moved to a new school. Before, "multiple Intelligences," you gave me confidence that being "Kinesthetically Smart," was a gift. You inspired me to become an Elementary P.E. teacher, to help other children to become confident in their bodies and skin. Thank-you, for being a good role model!

Claudia

Dear Mrs. Hopewood,

Thank-you, for being so good at your craft, being a 4th grade teacher. You shined your light on my ability to learn. You let us learn at our own pace and I now know you were decades ahead of your time. You literally were the teacher I wanted to grow up to be. And so I strive.

Your student always, Sally.

Thank-you, Mrs. King,

You were my favorite teacher at Burke Elementary. Thanks for the wonderful plays you had us learn and perform. I still remember songs from Hansel and Gretel and Snow White. All that memorizing was good!

Marcia

Dear Senora Bausch,
You were the best teacher I had in high school. Although I wasn't the best speaker of Espanol in the class you always encouraged me and I really had to earn that B+. It felt good to work hard for something. I didn't realize it then, but I do now. Also, when I saw you after graduation you genuinely encouraged my teaching career!

Thank-you, Marica

Dear Fr Harold Imamshah,

Thank-you! You were the one who challenged and encouraged me and left a permanent positive impact on my life!

Michaele

Dear Mrs. Forsyth,

You instilled a love of reading in me that I still have today. In second grade you read us a chapter each day of the book, *Heidi*. You read us many other books, but I remember this one vividly.

Thank-you, Diane

Dear Mr. Issac,

You were my High School government teacher in Charlotte, Michigan in the 50s. I still remember how you stretched out your arm in front of us each morning and said, "The Outstretched hand and the inverted Eyeball." (I am still not quite sure what you meant...) You made us read three newspapers or newsmagazines and give a report about what we read. I hated it, but I learned a lot. Your class was challenging, but I liked you because you treated us like adults!

Thank-you,
Rosalie

Dear Mr. McCallen,

I moved to your class in second grade and you welcomed me greatly. You were exuberant and fun. I learned to color in the lines, going the same way, and factor X factor equals product. We said it over and over. You were full of love and acceptance and I am proud to say I know you still 40 years later. I aspire to be you and influence the "Newbies," as you did me. I adore you!

Much love and Respect, Erin Grier

Dear Mrs. King,

You were my mother and my teacher in the 5th grade. You didn't spoil me and made me do my school work. I love you as my mother, but I didn't like you to teach me because you gave me so much work and wouldn't give me any special favors! I know that many students did love you, mom because you were a great teacher, just not for me!

Love, Linda

Dear Elizabeth,

You so wonderfully embraced the differences in all of your students! You made learning fun and I saw how cool it could be to be a teacher. Thank-you, for seeing what was behind the quiet, little second grader. Thank-you for understanding my love of jelly bracelets and Madonna. Thank-you for making my time at the Children's School something I will remember forever!

Love, Ann-Marie

Dear Mrs. Weller,

Thank-you, for realizing that I had test anxiety when I got the answers right in class, but was not doing so well on tests. You spent every lunch before a test with me drilling me so I wouldn't choke and had me correct any wrong answer and turn it back in because you, "knew I knew!" I got a B+ and passed my AP test because of you. I also learned not to give up on myself and to ask for help when I needed it!

Love, Tabatha

Acknowledgments

A Tribute to My Parents

I have been blessed to be surrounded by Dream Teachers all of my life. I was raised by two of them. My mother, Maxine Housler, was a beloved teacher to hundreds of children throughout her career. She started teaching in a little one room country school. I remember her coming home after work with her basket full of papers to check and sitting each evening at the card table in the living room working while the family watched TV. I enjoyed going to school with her to help her to get it set up for the new school year. The children in her classroom loved her and so many of them came to her 90th birthday party to see her that my sisters and I were amazed. She inspired me to become a teacher and was a living example of a Dream Teacher.

My father, Leon Housler, was an amazing, Renaissance, man. At the age of 40 he decided to change careers. He sold the cattle on our farm and went to Michigan State University. He loved to read, he enjoyed studying. He worked hard to complete his Bachelor's Degree to become a teacher in less than three years. He taught History and Speech at Maple Valley High School while he continued his education. He completed his Master's Degree at Michigan State and his Education Specialist Degree at University of Michigan. He later became the principal of the school that he taught, which was actually located in Nashville, Michigan, the town where he grew up. My dad loved to learn, and he shared his passion with the young people he taught. I was always proud of my dad, and he was a living example to me of what it takes to make your dreams come true!

Thank-you to Karen Krey and Vickie Winfield

Dear Vickie and Karen,

I have been double blessed to have two wonderful friends like you! Your passion for children and teaching is contagious and it is obvious in the work that you do in schools. You have inspired me to be a better educator. You have motivated me to continue my work as an educator to provide support to schools. You have also encouraged me and supported me through the process of writing this book. You are both Dream Teachers, that have not only achieved the dream for yourself, but helped others to become Dream Teachers.

Thank-you, to both of you for your inspiration as you patiently read each chapter to provide me with feedback and ideas to make this book a valuable tool for teachers. Each time I received your comments and feedback I anxiously went back and added your thoughts and ideas. You have literally breathed life into this book and for that I will be eternally grateful. Together we have created a book that teachers can use as a handbook to help them to become a Dream Teacher. Hopefully, the work that we have done together will impact generations of students to come!

Love, Becky

Thank-you to the Dream Teachers!

Special thanks to all the Dream Teachers in the United States, Abu Dhabi, Malaysia, England and Australia that helped to inspire this book! You are amazing and children from all over the world are lucky to have you as their teachers!

Dear Dream Teachers,

I have enjoyed our time together during the process of writing this book. Our Facebook Group, Dream Teachers, was the perfect forum for sharing our experience with each other. Thank-you for your patience as you answered questions for me to add to the "Tips from the Pros" section in each chapter. Your first-hand experience and knowledge is valuable to developing teachers. I learned so much from each one of you and you constantly gave me ideas that I actually used in the book. So please, think of this book as "our" book, because I couldn't have done it without you!

Becky

Dream Teachers

Ann-Marie Brown Trent—Teacher, 19 years, 1st grade, Atlanta, Georgia

Carole Kamerman—Teacher, Instructional Specialist, 37 years, Kalamazoo Public Schools

Claudia Champion Woodhouse—Teacher, 32 years, Grades K–4, Gaylord, Michigan
Vickie Winfield, Teacher and Principal, 40 years, Grades 1–6, Kalamazoo Public Schools
Marcy Peak—20 years, Licensed Professional Counselor, Director of Diversity and Community Outreach, Western Michigan University, Kalamazoo, Michigan
Lynne Mullane—Teacher and Principal, 37 years, High School, New South Wales, Australia
Mick Mullane—Teacher, 37 years, Primary School, New South Wales, Australia
John Henderson—Teacher, Education Specialist, 35 years, United Kingdom and UAE
Sharon Ferrar—Teacher, 23 years, Middle School Math and Science, Atlanta, Georgia
Karen Krey—Education Consultant, ICLE, Wisconsin
Krista Reilly—Teacher, 23 years, Atlanta Public Schools
Chelsea Adebayo—10 years, Grade 2–3, Atlanta Public Schools
Katie Carlson—Teacher, Atlanta Public Schools
Katie O'Toole—Teacher, Atlanta Public Schools
Eliza de Bruyn—Teacher, United Arab Emirates
Tina Williams—Teacher, ESOL, Atlanta Public Schools
Dawn-Marie Kahler—Teacher, 26 years, Grades 5–8, Kalamazoo Public Schools
Isabel Marsh—Teacher, 8 years, Dual Immersion Spanish Kindergarten, Atlanta Public Schools
Gail Lovely—Education Consultant, ICLE, Friendswood, Texas
Jenny Lockwood—Teacher, 14 years, Atlanta Public Schools
Kim Davidson—Teacher, 30 years, Grades 1–3
Erin Grier—"Ms. Egg" Sub and Para Pro-Atlanta, 3 years, Public Schools
Hannah-Hart Martin—Teacher, 12 years, Atlanta Public Schools
Marion Marks—Teacher, School Consultant, 20 years, United Kingdom and UAE
Jean Schmeichel—Teacher, Administrator, 45 years, Michigan, Illinois, Kansas
Jane Cisneros—Teacher, 29 years, Atlanta Public Schools
Gillian Bristol—Teacher, 20 years, Washington D.C. and UAE
Panzee Walker—Math Consultant, Education Consultant, Teacher Mentor, 20+ years, United States and UAE.

To My Readers,

If you would like to join my Facebook Group, Dream Teachers, please send a request. This will be a great forum for us to share our successes, ideas, and ask questions. If you would like to contact me, please email me at: beckyhunt1@me.com. I would love to hear about your Dream Classroom, and get feedback from you about the process. I hope that my book has been a helpful tool for you!

Thank-you so much for making the decision to be a teacher. I would like to support you and your school in any way that I can. Please don't hesitate to contact me. Good Luck on your journey. You won't have to walk it alone!

Sincerely,
Becky Hunt

www.beckyhunt.net
Atlanta, Georgia